p. 30-90

THE MEANING OF LOVE

EDITED BY
Ashley Montagu

GREENWOOD PRESS, PUBLISHERS
WESTPORT, CONNECTICUT

Library of Congress Cataloging in Publication Data

Montagu, Ashley, 1905-
　　The meaning of love.

　　Reprint of the ed. published by Julian Press, New York.
　　1. Love.　I.　Title.
[BD436.M6　1974]　　　177'.7　　　　72-11335
ISBN 0-8371-6656-X

Copyright 1953 by Ashley Montagu

Originally published in 1953 by The Julian Press, Inc., New York

Reprinted with the permission of Ashley Montagu

Reprinted in 1974 by Greenwood Press, a division of Williamhouse-Regency Inc.

Library of Congress Catalog Card Number 72-11335

ISBN 0-8371-6656-X

Printed in the United States of America

Contents

Introduction	v
The Origin and Meaning of Love by *Ashley Montagu*	3
On Loving by *Lawrence K. Frank*	25
Maternal Love by *Leon J. Saul, M.D.*	49
Love in Healthy People by *A. H. Maslow*	57
The Power of Creative Love by *Pitirim A. Sorokin* and *Robert C. Hanson*	97
Sexual Love—Man Toward Woman by *O. Spurgeon English, M.D.*	163
Sexual Love—Woman Toward Man by *Marynia F. Farnham, M.D.*	179
Love of Friends by *Alvin Johnson*	195
The Love of Mankind by *H. M. Kallen*	211
The Love of God by *James Luther Adams*	233

Introduction

Many books have been written about "love," but few have been concerned with love as the motivating and driving force which it constitutes in human society (even in the face of its many contemporary aberrations and distortions). Human beings have used the word "love" for a very long time. In the Western World, particularly through the vehicle of the Christian tradition, the word has perhaps been more frequently used or, at least, thought, than in any other culture area—more frequently and in more senses. Yet how many persons in our culture have understood the *true* meaning of this word? The true meaning, what is it? That is the question which this book will attempt to answer. I believe that it is extremely important for the world as a whole that we discover or perhaps re-discover the genuine meaning of love.

To help liberate the love that is within them, to enable more people to understand, feel, and enjoy the great power that is within them, the great need which they have to give and receive love, is the primary purpose of the present volume.

Everyone agrees that love is good. In a world characterized by a great deal of disagreement there would probably be a considerable amount of agreement as to the high value of love. Indeed, we are frequently told that the hope of the world consists in drawing upon the resources contained in man's capacity for love.

We are here confronted with something which has an

enormous amount of consensual validation, and which no one would willingly forego. Yet of all man's capacities, love is the one which has least fulfilled his expectations of it. Hate has been much more successful on this score. Inventiveness and the skill to master the physical world have rarely disappointed man's high hopes of his capacities. Nothing seems to be failing on such a magnificent scale as that which man claims he values most.

Why? How?

Inquiring into the various meanings of love, we may obtain a clue as to why man does not secure satisfaction from his loving. Apparently, for all its idealistic definition, there is something faulty with the way he has learned to love or been taught it, which is the reverse side of the same medal. Does the problem lie in *what* he has been taught or *how* he has learned it? Or has he learned something else and confused it with "love"? The problem then becomes one of understanding what he is doing and at least calling the results by another name. It is highly desirable that we clear up the confusion, for as Francis Bacon remarked, "Truth grows more readily out of error than out of confusion."

One of the reasons why we have been so confused in achieving a better understanding of love is that in practically every aspect of "loving" what we encounter is not so much the expression of love as the expression of the frustration of love. The fundamental dynamic implicit in love has apparently been by-passed. It has become a commandment rather than an emotion, a feeling and a need. It is a "must"—a "should"—or an "I can't." This is apparent, in our culture, in the way in which a child is required to feel toward its parents, and the parents are expected to feel toward the child, all the way down the line to "how" a man is "supposed" to feel toward a woman and vice versa (not how he feels but how he "should" feel).

In our time what is called mass neurosis is variously ascribed to failure to receive the proper affection in childhood, emotional immaturity, failure to achieve object love, and the like. In all these conditions the basic factor is identified with love. Love is apparently the goal which human beings set for themselves as the way to happiness; its lack is the source of all evil. Few persons in the cultures of the Western World seem to have been loved enough or to be able to love anyone else to their satisfaction.

What about this much-abused word? It has variously been identified with the lust of the body or with the voice of the spirit; as possessiveness or altruism; as an instinct or an emotion; as a drive or a mystical quality. The word has been used in so many senses, and within the last hundred and fifty years has become so increasingly debased, that Gresham's Law can be said to have been in effect for too long a time: the bad meanings of the word having driven out the good.

In this book an attempt is made to restore something of the true meaning of love to the understanding of human beings and the vocabulary of human expression.

Each of the contributors to this volume—with the exception of the editor—is distinguished not only as an outstanding authority on the subject on which he writes, but as, what is perhaps even more important, a person who has fulfilled Freud's specifications for mental health, namely, the ability to love and the ability to work. It is principally for this reason that those who have made this volume what it is were invited to contribute to it. It has been a most

INTRODUCTION

pleasant task to work with the contributors to this book, and I take this opportunity to express my heartfelt thanks to each of them.

To Mr. Arthur Ceppos, President of the Julian Press, I am indebted for having invited me to undertake the creation of this volume, for it was he who first conceived the idea for the book. I am also indebted to him for many courtesies shown me during the progress of the work.

Ashley Montagu

Princeton, N. J.
2 February 1953

The Origin and Meaning of Love

Ashley Montagu

The Origin and Meaning of Love

Ashley Montagu

> "It is strange that men will talk of miracles, revelations, inspirations, and the like, as things past, while love remains."
> THOREAU

What is love? Since we are going to talk about its origin, perhaps we ought to begin by defining what it is that we are going to talk about the origin of. To begin with a definition may be helpful, although it cannot be too often repeated that definitions can be meaningful only at the end of an inquiry and not at the beginning. So let us, for the time being, be content with the dictionary definition of love as "a feeling of deep regard, fondness, and devotion; deep affection, usually accompanied by yearning or desire for; affection between persons of the opposite sex, more or less founded on or combined with desire or passion." Perhaps when we have concluded our discussion, we shall understand more profoundly what these words mean.

It has often been the case in medicine that our first clues to the understanding of the functioning of normal processes have been discovered by a study of the pathological or disordered function. One of the most enlightening ways of studying the nature and meaning of love is to study the history of persons incapable of exhibiting it.

When such persons are studied, it is invariably found that something was lacking in their mother's relationship to them. The mother had either died when they were very young; the mother had been bedridden and unable to attend to them for a prolonged period of time; the mother had been absent for one reason or another for long periods of time during their infancy; or the mother had been actively hostile or else frankly inadequate, and so on. These findings are set out with great clarity in Dr. John Bowlby's admirable analysis (for the World Health Organization) of the research data entitled *Maternal Care and Mental Health* (Columbia University Press, New York, 1951). In all these cases the children were starved of love during either the whole or some critical period of their development. Such children, if they manage to survive—for many of them die for want of nothing more than love—will exhibit as adolescents and as adults an inability to function affectively, a marked want of affection. Such persons are characterized by the fact that they leave most people with whom they come into "contact" quite "cold." Being "cold" themselves, they fail to elicit warmth in others. When introduced, they are likely to deposit a cold, dangling, boneless fish in your hand, and it is your responsibility to do something with it. Or having become aware of their own lack of warmth, they are apt to overcompensate for it, in many instances, by crushing the bones of your hand in such a manner as to bruise your fingers.

As children they cause their parents much worry owing to their want of affection, selfishness, lack of consideration for others, and jealousy of their siblings. As adults they tend to become difficult people who cannot get along with anyone. They are soon recognized as "cold fish," "selfish," "egotistical," and uncompromisingly ruthless in their human relationships. They seem to behave as if they neither cared for other people nor for what other people think about them. But this is only appearance, for in reality more than anything else in the world they want to care for other people and have other people care for them. These are the people who are suffering from "primary affect hunger," as David Levy has called it, the hunger for love. Wishing to be loved, they attempt again and again to elicit love from other persons, but not having been adequately loved themselves they have never learned how to love properly; or to put it more accurately, they have been so starved and undeveloped in their capacity to love by the privations of love which they have suffered in infancy and childhood that they are unable to love as adults. Such persons are lacking in social competence, and their incapacity may express itself in a manner all the way from an unfortunate lack of warmth, social inadequacy, and social disoperativeness, to juvenile delinquency in childhood and criminal behavior as an adult.

Such persons require our profoundest and most sympathetic understanding, for they are generally the innocent victims of a lack-love childhood—human beings who have been deprived of the birthright of humanity, namely, the loving care of a mother. But for the moment their interest for us here is clinical; they teach us something by the very absence of the traits—as well as the presence of others—they exhibit. Why do we call the people I have described "unloving?" It is because they are peculiar both for the traits they exhibit and those they do not.

The "unloving" person is cold; we say that he lacks "warmth." When he shakes hands there are no "vibrations," he doesn't seem to operate on the same "wavelength" as other people, one "can't get under his skin," he doesn't cooperate, and he is too selfish to make a good companion. Such a person's human relationships have a certain shallowness of feeling about them, a condition rendering it extremely difficult, if not impossible, for him to enter deeply into another person's feelings; he seems to be almost entirely lacking in the capacity to put himself in the other person's place. He is a person who is forever attempting to make withdrawals from a bank in which he has made no deposits. Hence, to change the metaphor, he can cruise about on the sea of human relationships with the greatest of ease, abandoning one "love affair" for another, or terminating one marriage after another, without batting so much as an emotional eyelid. Lacking the capacity for deep feeling toward others, he frequently makes "intellect" do service for warmth—usually unsuccessfully, and largely as a mechanism for rationalizing away his incapacity to love. He will often deplore the display of affection as vulgar or ill-bred or insincere.

Failing in his quest for love, such a person will often try to find it through the quest for power. The power may take the form of status or wealth; in either case the idea seems to be that by acquiring power one will have all that love can give, or else by using power one may acquire love. Unfortunately for such persons it turns out that power is a very poor substitute for love, and love has never yet been acquired by power. In the course of their quest for power as an image of love such persons, by virtue of their human shallowness and social incompetence, are likely to do a great deal of personal and social damage. Concerned with catering to their own needs, they are not much interested in attending to the needs of others. Since their great driving force is a need for love which has been consistently frustrated and thus turned, in part, into hatred, the end they seek may be love, even though the means to its attainment may be hateful. They may justify this to themselves because by such means those who have prevented them from receiving love may be symbolically punished even though it be through the persons of the guiltless. One may suspect that many who believe in the doctrine of the end justifying the means belong to this class of persons.

The person who has been adequately loved, but conditioned in a competitive milieu, may occasionally fall from grace and resort to evil means in order to attain some end, but such behavior in a person of this kind is likely to be exceptional and at the cost of some wrestling with his conscience. In the unloving person, on the contrary, such conduct is likely to be the rule rather than the exception, and since his conscience contains little or nothing of the structure of love within it, such inhibitions as he may experience are those which are imposed upon him from without rather than from within. The adequately loved and loving person, even in a competitive culture, finds it difficult to employ hateful means to attain "good" ends. The unloving person experiences little or no difficulty at all.

Now, among the many things which should be clear to the reader concerning the character of the unloved and unloving person is the fact that his particular kind of "hatefulness" is somehow very closely related to his incapacity to love. And indeed it is, for his "hatefulness" is the result of the fact that he was inadequately loved during his infancy and childhood. The fact is that his hatred is a form of love. Such a statement may appear to be something of a paradox, but only because in the cultures of the Western World we have failed to understand the true significance of love and hate. Hatred is nothing but love frustrated. Hatred is not love, but it is not far from it. It is not that the child is born with the emotion of love and the emotion of hate, but rather he is born with the emotion of love, and when that emotion is consistently and strongly enough frustrated, it turns into hatred or aggressiveness—two different words for very nearly the same thing. Aggressiveness may appear to be hatred, and hatred may appear to be aggressive, without either in fact being so, though, of course, aggressiveness and hatred may be given a content of active hostility which may be very damaging indeed both to the subject and to the object of them. Such facts make it nonetheless understandable that aggressiveness (which term I shall hereafter use as equivalent to or including hate) can be considered as a form of love.

While, strictly speaking, it is more accurate to regard aggressiveness as a deformed aspect of love, I think it is more meaningful to speak of it as a form of love, the inverse of love, for when we speak of aggressiveness in this manner it helps us better to understand its true meaning.

It is becoming increasingly clear to investigators of human development that the infant is born not alone with the desire to be loved but also with the desire to love. It is *not* born aggressive, "sinful," "naughty," or "hostile," or any of the other unattractive traits of which it has been accused. It wants to be loved and to love. When it is not loved, its expectation of love is frustrated, and one of the means to which it will invariably resort in order to secure love is aggressiveness. Aggressiveness is a technique or means of securing love. Aggressiveness is an attempt to compel love—

it is the clutching at straws in a sea of human indifference, and the clutching is sometimes pretty vigorous. The infant is born in a state of complete dependency, expecting to be supported in all its needs by "others." Not that at birth it has a consciousness of "others" or even of expectation, but it *does* have needs and it "expects" to have them satisfied, "expects" in the sense that it is painfully disappointed when those needs are not satisfied. When its needs are not adequately satisfied, it experiences a failure of support and becomes anxious and insecure. Fundamentally that is what anxiety is, a fear of lack of support, a fear of separation from the mother, a fear of the loss of love. Insecurity is but another word, a doubleton, for the same thing. Under such conditions the infant's desire to love and be loved may reach such a state of unrelieved pressure or tension that it will then take the form of attempting to compel the attention of "others" in order to elicit the required love from them.

Because these facts are not generally understood, we treat such aggressive behavior in the same manner as we do hostility, combativeness, and violence; we call such behavior "bad" and we prescribe punishments for it, and by so doing we turn the "bad" situation which we have created into a really bad one. I think it highly probable that where human beings are involved in the normal interpersonal situations of life, whenever aggressiveness appears, it is either a direct or an indirect expression of the desire to love and be loved. There already exists a great deal of evidence in support of this interpretation of the nature of aggression; research now being conducted and future researches are likely to provide the finally conclusive evidence.

We can now begin to see, I think, something of the meaning of love by considering the responses of the person who has suffered from the want of it.

(To love is to be affectively related to other people and to oneself in such a manner as to render them and ourselves more secure, to convey to others the feeling that we are "all for" them, that we are there to support and cooperate with them.) This, however hard he may try, the unloved-unloving person cannot do. He wants to be and do all these things, but he can't. As one such person tragically remarked to me some years ago: "I know it's all there, but it's as if a wall of concrete surrounded my heart, and desperately hard as I try to express it, the warmth won't come out." Such a person by being inadequately loved has been inadequately related both to himself and to other persons. In other words, the love relationship is essentially a social relationship. By social we mean the interaction between persons in a manner which confers survival benefits upon them. That, then, is to say that to love means to minister to, to satisfy, the needs of other persons, and by this means to relate them to ourselves. Insofar as this means anything to the infant, it means that its dependence and specific needs must be satisfied if it is to survive—and it *wants* to survive.

Now, we know from the study of overprotected children, as also from the study of children who have had all their purely physical needs satisfied, that the satisfaction of physical needs alone is not enough, for the greatest of all needs of the human being is the need for love, the experiencing of the feeling conveyed by "others" that one is wanted, needed, liked, appreciated, valued, and deeply involved with the "other" or "others." One wants to feel that one is in interdependent relationship with "others," bound up with them, supported and supporting. To be cut off from others is death. Man is born for participation, and there is no pain more unbearable than the feeling of being alone. If I were asked to give a brief description of the meaning of love on the basis of the facts we have thus far discussed, I would say that it is the feeling of being "all for" others, and also as part of this the feeling that others are "all for" you, and that if the others are not, it is because they don't know any better, not because they don't want to be "all for" you. The one word which describes this feeling is *interdependence*.

All the evidence bearing upon this matter with which I am acquainted suggests that there is one word which better than any other indicates what love really is. It is *interdependence*. Interdependence, the state of depending upon each other, is the state of all living things. Without interdependence no living group of organisms could survive, and insofar as any group of organisms departs in its functioning from the requirement of interdependence, to that extent does it become malfunctional and disoperative. This is a more particular statement of the general principle that the probability of survival of individuals or groups of living things increases with the degree with which they harmoniously adjust themselves to each other and to their environment. "Interdependence" states, I think, more sharply the essence of what has been called "the harmony of nature" than does the word "harmony."

What is the origin of interdependence? This, of course, is to ask what is the origin of love?

THE ORIGIN OF LOVE

In what follows it should be clearly understood that insofar as the lower organisms are concerned we can only conjecture the significance of many facts. With respect to inorganic matter we can at best only speculate as to the meaning of the facts. But it should also be clearly understood that both for the world of inorganic matter and that of organic matter there are certain facts which are ineluctably clear, provable, and available for checking. In the case of man as man, the evidence is now largely beyond question; it is neither conjectural nor speculative—the relations obtaining between the facts are clear and their meaning is as verifiable as any objectively verifiable datum of experience.

THE INORGANIC

It is possible, even probable, that the most primitive, that is to say, earliest and most unorganized representation of what ultimately develops as the state or condition of love is the tendency found in all matter to cohere, to stay together. When any bit of matter is broken down into its smallest particles, the particles which constitute the nucleus of the atom, it is found that they have a complex relationship to one another. And when everything is said and done, and all our final analyses are in, and the equations written, the relations to one another of the particles constituting the atom appear to be best described by the one word "cooperation." It may, indeed, be said that it is the cooperation of the particles of the nucleus of the atom which maintains the form and substance of the atom. And it may further be said that it is possible for matter to assume the enormous variety of complex forms which it does because of the cooperation not only of atoms of the same kind but among atoms of different kinds. This holds true for those more complexly organized forms of matter known as molecules. Molecules are constituted of atoms and may vary from one atom, as in hydrogen, to many thousands, as in the protein molecule known as serum albumin, in which there are nearly ten thousand atoms, nearly five thousand of them hydrogen, three thousand carbon, one thousand oxygen, seven hundred nitrogen, and forty sulfur. There are very few forms of life which could exist without the presence of this molecule. That this molecule itself exists is the result of the contact and interdependence between the intramolecular atoms, and between the particles of the nuclei of the constitutive atoms. The "social" behavior of molecules has been described by Professor George Scatchard of the Massachusetts Institute of Technology. It is no part of my task, even if I were competent to do so, to describe the physics of interdependence in atoms and molecules. The fact is that such an interdependence exists, and it can be observed and verified.

In the inorganic world the interdependence exists at a somewhat less complex level of integration than in the organic world, but it exists; and there can be little doubt that an evolutionary relationship exists between one and the other. The suggestion is that the complex state of interdependence exhibited by human beings has some part of its origin in the tendency of all matter, inorganic and organic, to *interdepend*. For the purposes of our discussion this is an unnecessary suggestion, but I have nevertheless thought the facts of sufficient interest to dwell upon them here, however briefly. I believe that they have their importance in our discussion, and I hope they will cause the reader to dwell upon their possible significance, for again, the suggestion is that the tendency of all things universally is toward interdependence. The further suggestion is that this tendency is an inherent property of all matter and finds its most complex and most highly developed form in living matter. In inorganic matter the interdependence is seen in the pattern of atoms of which it is constituted, while in organic matter this interdependence becomes more complex owing to the greater complexity of organization of the organic as compared with the inorganic. And that is one of the reasons why the term "organism" is one of the happiest in the whole vocabulary of biology. The organism is an organized system of interdependencies. And by "a complex organism" we mean just this: that the more complex the organism, the more complexly organized is its system of interdependencies.

THE ORGANIC—THE ORGANISM

It is simpler to perceive the origins of love and its meaning when we look for them in the organic world, especially in organized forms of life. Let us take for our observations the familiar single-celled organism of classroom and textbook biology: the amoeba. The amoeba will serve as our representative example of what goes on in all single cells, whether they be unicellular organisms or parts of a multicellular organism.

An amoeba grows, that is to say, it increases in size, and during the progress of its growth it eventually reaches a stage at which it reproduces itself. This statement has been made about amoebae and other cells an untold number of times, but what seems to have escaped the attention of most observers—largely, it is to be supposed, because they were not interested in this particular aspect of the phenomenon—is that the reproductive process constitutes the clue to our understanding of the nature of love and the nature of social life.

When one observes an amoeba about to reproduce under the microscope, one observes first that there is a duplication of the nucleus, so that there are now two nuclei. This is followed by an invagination of the cell membrane at the upper and lower poles of the amoeba. For all practical and theoretical purposes there are now two cells within a single membrane. Whatever affects the one affects the other. Both cells are in the closest relation of interdependence, and it is during this relation and as a result of this state of interdependence that the pattern of all interorganismic relations is determined. So that when the invaginations of the membrane have deepened sufficiently for them to unite and the two cells to become separated, the separation is only one in terms of a semi-permeable membrane; they still remain together as part of one another's environment. When one carefully observes such amoebae, one finds that they tend to remain together. Where one encounters one amoeba, one will find others. It is here being suggested that the tendency for amoebae to aggregate is in origin related to the fact that each amoeba once formed a part of another amoeba, and that during the process of reproduction the emerging "daughter" cell acquires the "habit" of dependence upon the "maternal" cell,* and also the "habit" of interdependence. It is al-

---

* Whether one speaks of "maternal" and "daughter" cells or "sister" cells depends upon which school of philosophical biology one belongs to. Actually the difference is as between Tweedledum and Tweedledee, although when one thinks out the consequences of the two terminological viewpoints serious differences *can* arise. I belong to the "maternal-daughter" cell school.

ready possible for biophysicists to study and measure some of these interdependent relationships, but thus far they are able to express them only in physical terms.

It is in the reproductive relationship with its profound interdependencies that one may perceive the origin and meaning of love—to give reciprocally, which means also to receive reciprocally; to give mutual support and security, to cooperate, to confer survival benefits upon each other. A tree which stands alone is not likely to do as well in the long run as a tree which is in close association with other trees. The branches of adjacent trees give each other support, and in the strong wind, while the solitary tree would be blown over, the associated trees would stand together. This is an example of the obvious kind of physical support which living things give one another, but there are intangible supports which they give one another, and these intangibles, I suspect, differ in man from those which are operative in other living creatures, not so much in kind as in degree. Animals which would die as the result of certain noxious stimuli, were they alone, survive much longer when the same stimuli are received under group conditions. Soldiers, under combat conditions, show a high frequency of psychiatric breakdown when they have been trained in the usual heartless way. The "it may break your mother's heart, but it won't break mine" type of training which the soldier has, in the past, received has left him on the battlefield pretty much to his own resources. Under such conditions "combat fatigue" is of frequent occurrence. On the other hand, the soldier who has been trained in such a manner as to be made to feel an interdependent part of the group, who becomes bound to his fellow soldiers by close emotional ties, who knows that whatever happens he will always find support and not be left to fight his battle alone, is very unlikely to succumb to "combat fatigue." The feeling of membership in a group gives him the feeling of "belongingness," of "togetherness," protecting him against fear and providing support for his emotional needs. Captain Albert J. Glass, who conducted the study on "combat exhaustion," concludes that "a member of an adequately led combat unit has an increased resistance to mental breakdown because of the emotional and actual support provided by the group. The failure of such an environmental support is the major cause of combat exhaustion."

Wherever organisms are interacting in a related manner, they are conferring survival benefits upon each other. Whenever organisms interact in an unrelated manner, as "independents," they confer negative survival benefits upon themselves and upon their fellows. "Relatedness," "togetherness," "belongingness"—this is the triad of complex feelings which the person must have if he is to be a loving person, if he is to be mentally healthy. It seems to be in the nature of living organisms to be related, together, and to belong, and it is suggested that the evidence indicates that these states have their origins in the very organization of living matter, and become more integratively complex and developed as the organism becomes so, reaching their highest integration at the human level.

Love has its remotest origins, then, in the organization of matter, in the integrative, essentially cooperative relations of the particles constituting matter. At the level of living matter this integrative, cooperative relationship between the particles of matter becomes more complexly organized. In the process of reproduction the interdependence of the functioning units of the organism becomes extended to the interdependence of functioning organisms. At the level of human symbolic thought, at the level of human culture, that is to say, the way of life of a people, this interdependence assumes a complexity varying with the degree of complexity of each culture. The signs and symbols and meanings of love become increasingly more complex and abstract, and increase in number. Evidences of love may take almost any form, and may vary considerably in different cultures; but whatever the variety of forms which the signs, symbols, and other evidence of love may take, I believe it will be found upon analysis that they are all traceable to the need for the kind of love which is biologically determined, predetermined, to exist between mother and infant.

All babies are born with the need to be loved and to love, and this need remains with them throughout their lives, whether they have actually been loved or not. As a consequence of not having been adequately loved during the first six years of their lives, such persons may not know how to love, but it remains a fact that they want to love as well as to be loved, but that they simply do not know how. The biologically determined fundamental relationship which would naturally exist between human beings, if it were not inhibited by the kind of frustrations to which children are exposed in our culture (as well as in others) in the name and cause of discipline, is the love relationship. It is primary nature, and it should also be sound nature for human beings to love one another. As it is, primary nature remains striving to love and be loved, while second nature often puts calculated restraints upon such striving and erects certain barriers deliberately designed to prevent its expression—all this because the true meaning of love has not been understood.

To inhibit or prevent the expression of love is to do violence to the needs, to the structure, and to the functioning of the organism. To love and to be loved is as necessary to the organism as the breathing of air. Insofar as the organism fails in loving, it fails in living, for to live and love is, for a human being, the equivalent of healthy living. To live as if to live and love were one is not simply an ideal to be achieved, but a potentiality to be realized, a destiny to be fulfilled.

As our knowledge of the nature of man increases, it becomes increasingly evident that the pattern of love which all human beings undeviatingly require and which they desire to follow is the pattern of love which exists between mother and child. In every human being something of the maternal and something of the child in relation to the mother remains, and in order to love and be loved this is necessary and highly desirable. To the extent to which women succeed or do not succeed in adequately loving their children, the boys and girls become inadequately loving men and women. The men then become inadequately loving fathers, and the women go on producing inadequately loved children, who perpetuate this truly vicious cycle.

It is not an accident, we may suspect, that Christianity has had such a wide appeal, for here we have a religion with the central figure a father-image of love, a father who loves his children so much that he is even willing to sacrifice his only begotten son for them. Sons who have been sacrificed by their own fathers and who, as fathers themselves, may sacrifice their own sons, understandably find something attractive and satisfying about such a theology. For here one can at once have a father who is genuinely a father of love, a father whom one wished one's own father could have been, together with a filial relationship which is reminiscent of one's own, and which may unconsciously be realized in relation to one's son.

Women, it may be suggested, have found the identification with Mary and her relation to God and to Christ far from unsatisfying. Men have created not only God in their own image, but they have also projected their views of women and of children, particularly their sons, upon the screen of Christian belief in the images of Mary and of Christ. Both women and men have found the projection satisfying because it describes real conditions which in reality they cannot face, but which, in the form of a religious system or a mythology, they can face and upon which they can dwell. Here the life of the gods is but the life of man writ large, the life of man as he is, as he would have himself be, as he aspires to be. "God is Love," "Love thy neighbor as thyself," "Do unto others as you would have them do unto you," the injunction to love little children—these are but the cries of children who were not adequately loved by their fathers, the cries of children who want to be loved, and who have created gods who will love them and whom they can love. "God the Father," the God of Love, is the god we have created to compensate for our unloving actual fathers; we may worship and we may pray to him, but the first and the last word that is on our lips is not "Father"—it is "Mother." God the Father is the projection of a desire for a loving father of whom we have been deprived. "Mother" is the reality which, more or less satisfactorily, we have known.

In the United States the tyrannical father of Europe has been replaced by a father who is a friend, who is kind, and who does not compete with one; hence, the rarity of the Oedipus complex in American men and the liberalizing of American religion as a sort of *gemütlich* social institution rather than as a place of worship of father-substitutes. But if one's own father is satisfactory, it would seem that the fathers of a great many other men and women are not, to judge from the state in which the world is at the present time. Men are too hostile; wars threaten death and destruction. There is too little love in the world. Feeling so, men and women are returning to religion in the hope that within the "bosom" of the church they may find that love and protection which may not only give them what their parents and their fellows decline to give, but which somehow may help solve the problem of man's hostility.

The church can help, but it would be foolish to think that what the church has thus far failed to accomplish it will accomplish in this irreligious age. Modern churchmen are not unaware of this, and it is a happy augury in our time that they are beginning to join hands with the students of human nature so that they may better meet the requirements of women and men who seek to live as they should in this confused and confusing world. If scientists have much to teach churchmen, the men of religion have much to teach scientists. Each can learn from the other, and what, above all else, they can learn is that their purposes are the same: the discovery of the nature of nature, of which man is a part, with especial reference to the nature of man, so that man may best be helped to achieve that perfection of character which may make life for him on this earth the heaven that he has in the past projected unreachably above him.

The most important thing to realize about the nature of human nature is that the most significant ingredient in its structure is love. The church has long recognized this; scientists are beginning to realize it; but it will be the educators of the world to whom the task will fall not only of explaining the nature of love but of teaching its meaning to the citizens of future generations. When that time arrives, we shall for the first time in the history of the Western World have truly educated human beings among us.

On Loving

Lawrence K. Frank

On Loving

Lawrence K. Frank

Love is a mighty word and, like other abstract nouns, may be used for many and diverse purposes, with different meanings and varying intentions.

Over the centuries, bitter disputes have been frequent among theologians and philosophers about the meaning of love. More recently, psychologists and psychiatrists have focused their attention upon love and its role in human living.

But it is chiefly the poets, the dramatists, and the novelists who have interpreted the word love, each in a different way, providing the many meanings and sanctions for the diverse application of this mighty, but confusing, word.

It seems hopeless to look for any early end to these verbal confusions and semantic conflicts. But we may gain some understanding if we will turn from the abstract and always ambiguous noun, love, to the verb, to love, and consider what *loving* involves.

When we focus upon *loving* and recognize loving as a kind of interpersonal relationship, we may begin to see more clearly what this essential, if not uniquely, human pattern of conduct and feelings means. When it is approached as a dynamic process, we can understand the acute need of love, not only by the infant and child but by adolescents and by adults, since denial of love, as we are now discovering, may block the attainment of our human potentialities, stunt our personalities, and prevent our maturation.

But before we examine these interpersonal relations, we must first recognize the essential dynamics of human living, as contrasted with organic existence.

I

Nothing is so difficult for us to realize as that, as organisms, we exist and survive by continual intercourse with the geographical world of nature; we carry on our live activities as members of our society in the public social world. But as personalities we *live,* each in the *private world* of his own creation.

We become a human being by learning, from other humans, the selective awareness, the patterned perception, the ideas and beliefs and prescribed conduct required by our cultural traditions and our social order. We learn to live in a symbolic world of meanings and values, of goal-seeking and purposive striving, above all, of the many diversified and complicated interpersonal relationships in and through which we build up and maintain our *life space* and *feel* our way through life.

While it is hard for us to recognize this, it is even more difficult to realize that we, as personalities, are engaged continually in creating our highly individualized version of this symbolic world. We must actively and continuously invest every object, animal, situation and event, person and relationship, with the idiomatic meaning and the feelings which it has for us and which we attribute to or project into it. These meanings and many of these feelings are derived from and patterned by our cultural traditions as interpreted by parents, teachers, and other adults. But each of us warps, often distorts, and always individualizes them and also infuses them with the emotional significance, the feeling tones, mild or strong, that they have for us alone. Thus we create our "private worlds" by our selective awareness and projection of meanings and feelings into every experience.

We are reluctant to recognize this, or to accept it, because we are so anxiously concerned with conforming to the prescribed cultural-social norm. We must believe that we are normal, like everyone else; that we speak, think, act and feel like others; yet we want to be different; we know we are different, that each of us is an individual.

As Strode has suggested, it is as if each of us had a private radar set of our own; we send out our radar impulses into a world of indifferent makers, and as they come back we say, "Ah, that's the world," and we strive to make the world and other people conform to the meaning we have put into them.

This insight into our basic human personality is one of the major discoveries of recent times. For many years we shall be exploring the varied implications and consequences of this new understanding. But today we can confidently assert that each individual personality lives primarily by investing all situations and events, all persons and activities, with the meaning he has learned to give them, imputing to them the value, the significance, the highly individualized worth they have for him alone. And to each such experience the individual personality responds with the feelings, usually the chronic feelings of anxiety, guilt, resentment, affection, etc. which he idiomatically gives to all events and persons.

If anyone doubts this, he should recall the amazingly different cultures all over the world, where each group of people has developed its own traditional ideas and interpretations of nature and of man, with its own form of social order. Moreover, we should remember that only slowly and partially has man learned to see the so-called objective world, gradually replacing his naive beliefs and assumptions with those that are more credible, as we see in the history of science.

But even more compelling to this view is the daily experience of seeing others speak, act, and feel toward any event or situation in such highly idiomatic ways that so clearly indicate that each "sees" a different situation, interprets it in his own way, and reacts with feelings that are peculiarly his own.

As human beings we are the creators of the "private worlds" we live in and, by partially sharing these with others, we maintain our culture and social order. Our lives are oriented by these meanings and values that we attribute to all events and people. Indeed, human living, as distinguished from the organic existence which we enjoy along with other organisms, is essentially this process of putting meaning into situations, and responding to our own interpretations of their value and significance. Human living thereby becomes purposeful, since we act toward every event as the signal, sign, or symbol for the kind of patterned conduct we have learned as our way of dealing with the world of situations and other persons.

We interpret everything we are aware of as meaningful, having some significance or value, some emotional import to which we respond according to its meaning, as promising for the future or as threats or dangers. Often, and here we have recently gained a new insight, the feelings or emotional response we give to a situation or person may be not only inappropriate to, but conflicting with, the meaning according to which we act, thereby creating confusion for others and frustration for ourselves.

When we recognize this dynamic circular process of human living, we can begin to understand some of the baffling aspects of human conduct and especially of human relationship. We learn in childhood to give up our naive impulsive behavior, the unpatterned and often random reactions to the world, for the patterned conduct required by our culture and social order. Gradually we learn to deal with all situations purposively, according to their meaning. Through language we learn that everything has a name and a definition, and early in childhood we learn to deal with things and people according to their names and their meanings. Every event then becomes the sign or symbol, the antecedent to more remote or deferred goals for which we learn to strive, or as the symbols to which we respond with appropriate conduct.

Living becomes ever more purposive and goal-seeking as we recognize every event in terms of its significance for what is to happen or can be made to happen by our own manipulations and skillful contrivance. Immediate satisfactions are rejected for deferred consummations or for symbolic fulfillments that may become more valuable than actuality.

But human living is more than calculated exploitation of the environment by man's skillful hands and imaginative foresight. Man also has the capacity for esthetic experience, of responding to situations and persons, not as means to ends, or instruments for achieving his goals, but as events that give joy, delight, exaltation—those all-engrossing experiences that have no concern for the past nor the future but are focused by the immediate here and now.

Without this capacity for esthetic response, man would indeed be an industrious animal, the contriver of tools and techniques, but lacking the uniquely human experience of sheer, purposeless enjoyment when, if and for a brief interval, he can live most intensely and fully.

That is why we are so indebted to the artist, the poet, the musician, the dramatist, the novelist—all those whose creative imagination have enriched living by giving us the awareness and the perceptions that have enlarged and intensified our otherwise drab and meager experiences.

Human living is governed by the meaning of all experiences that each culture has developed and that each individual person idiomatically interprets in his own way, with feelings.

II

When we recognize this dynamic circular process of putting meaning into situations, and then responding to the meaning which we ourselves have invested or projected therein with the feelings that we bring to all experience, then we may begin to understand better some of the dynamics of loving.

For loving is a special manifestation of this basic human process that pervades all human living, but is uniquely exhibited in interpersonal relationship.

We are continually engaged in this process of investing people with meaning, imputing specific significance or worth to them, and then responding to our evaluations with more or less appropriate conduct. And we are continually responding to people with feelings of greater or less intensity of liking or disliking, of loving or hating, which we may or may not recognize.

In every social order each person has a certain status, rank, order, position, official or formal relationship to all others. Indeed, it is astonishing to reflect upon the number and variety of roles an individual is expected to fulfill, differing according to sex and with increasing age and widening activities. Our traditions, our social institutions, our families, all impress upon us the importance of playing these roles, carrying out their appropriate rituals and established practices, responding to others according to their status, rank, and position, and according to what is required or expected.

Much of our daily life becomes routinized by these prescribed patterns of relationships and reciprocal activities. Much of our daily conduct is focused upon dealing with others as potential aids or obstacles to the achievement of the goals we are seeking, so that we frequently instrumentalize people, using them, so to speak, for our own purposes so far as they are amenable or not too resistant. Or we attack and resist others who seem to oppose or block our attempts to achieve something.

But we also live by investing some persons with unusual significance and worth, imputing to these persons a special significance that is not governed by their usefulness or manipulatability. We attribute greatest worth to them; we see in them something that makes living more desirable and that fulfills our esthetic capacity for enjoyment of life.

Here we begin to see that if a person is lovable, we put

the lovableness into them, we invest them with the special qualities that we delight to behold, and then we act toward them as lovable, hoping to evoke reciprocally their loving response. If we are fortunate we establish a "virtuous circle" (as contrasted with the well-known "vicious circle"), where the more we impute lovableness to another and act toward him or her as lovable, the more that person becomes loving toward us.

Unless we recognize this highly idiomatic dynamic process, we cannot hope to understand the infinitely complex, subtle, and often baffling relationships that we create, and the frustrations, defeats, and often tragic conflicts they frequently engender.

Those who are reluctant to accept this highly individualized, dynamic circular process as the clue to the loving relationship should recall how often they have heard, or have themselves remarked, of a recently announced engagement or betrothal, "I can't see what she (or he) sees in that man (woman)." Naturally the outsider, viewing the engaged couple with more or less detachment, cannot possibly understand the meaning, the worth, the esthetic significance (apart from sexual attraction) which the engaged man and woman are attributing to each other.

Indeed, without an insightful understanding of the individual's personality, it is almost impossible to discover what peculiar idiomatic meaning each person in a relationship—not only of marriage but of parent-child, siblings, friendship, comrades—brings to these relationships.

But what is also difficult to understand is how often the relationship is not reciprocal, but continues as one persistently endows the other with value, going on loving with little or no response from the other. Here, indeed, we see this dynamic circular response exhibited as the loving individual, despite the lack of response and even in the face of outright rejection or sometimes cruel and brutal treatment, goes on loving the other, with no hope or expectation of return.

Loving, like all other aspects of this dynamic circular process of putting meaning into situations, has to be learned by experience. Thus, it is becoming clear that we can invest another with lovableness and respond with loving, only if we have earlier experienced being loved ourselves. We must have once been the focus of another's loving, have had the experience of being invested with worth, treated with tenderness, felt the warm concern and focused interest of someone, in order to be able to love another. We don't know how to love except by learning from being loved. That is why students of personality development and psychotherapeutics are emphasizing so strongly the crucial importance of loving the infant and child; also why they are telling us that so many of the neurotics and mentally disordered suffer from the inability to love. Indeed psychiatry and psychoanalysis have given us a new and powerful reinforcement for our age-old belief in the crucial significance of loving.

Again we are confronted with a profound insight of recent discovery, that we can be loving to another only if we love ourselves, feel friendly, lovable, to our own personalities. As Erich Fromm has emphasized, this challenges one of our long-established traditions: that we should devaluate and despise ourselves, as if out of self-rejection we can somehow develop the capacity to love and value others.

Perhaps we can find a much-needed clue to the essential

core of loving if we recognize that loving as here interpreted is an expression of generosity, a giving of ourselves, our interest, our concern, our tenderness—all that we as personalities can offer freely and generously to another.

Thus, in loving a person we are not using that person as means to an end, as an instrument for some purpose or goal which may be wholly alien to that person. In loving another, we spontaneously offer ourselves, our genuine and wholehearted admiration, devotion, tenderness, all the different expressions of our concern for the other.

To be generous, we now realize, one must be strong, with the strength and confidence that comes from inside, not from having power over others outside. And we also are discovering that being generous makes us stronger, gives us the feeling of self-confidence and the capacity to meet life more adequately because we can give to others and feel more adequate by so giving.

Thus we may say that when we love another we are attaining the strength we need to live fully as a human personality and to mature with the years. Indeed, marriage, child-bearing and rearing are the major opportunities for us to "grow up," to mature, to develop strength through the generous love and care we give to our spouse and our children.

As human personalities, within our "private world," we are often lonely and anxious, eager to be recognized and accepted by others. We can escape from our isolation only if we can genuinely communicate with another, which occurs when we are generous, outgoing, capable of investing another with lovableness, of loving that person and, by that loving, evoking a reciprocal response of loving from him or her.

When we do genuinely love another, we live and function more intensely and completely. We have a truly esthetic experience, of being more or less completely engrossed in that person, lifted out of ourselves and our usual self-centered preoccupations and reveries, because for the time we are giving to another and finding fulfillment in our generosity.

This direct, immediate response to another, with no thought of goals and purposes, no reflection, no anxiety over conformity to social requirements, is what gives esthetic experience its special significance as a renewal of living.

We see this extraordinary uplift and transformation dramatically occurring when, for the first time in their lives, the young man and woman begin to be concerned about the other, to give primacy to the welfare of each other, to feel exalted through the liberating experience of being generous, of loving and being loved.

Indeed, we may say that loving, in the sense here being interpreted, is probably *the* central core of the human personality, since in loving, the human capacity for this dynamic circular process is expressed more fully and intensely than in any other experience. Through loving we realize, in greater or less measure, one of our greatest human potentialities and thereby genuinely participate in living as a member of a human society.

If we think of loving as a dynamic circular process, a communication from one "private world" to another, we shall see that the sexual relationship between a man and a woman offers what Dr. James L. Plant called "another language" for such communication. What cannot be expressed adequately in words may be communicated with hands, lips, and the exquisitely sensitive genitals to give each other the experience of being valued and sexually fulfilled, essentially an esthetic experience. Again it is being revealed that for sexual fulfillment, generosity is essential, since only as the sex partners give each other the feeling of special worth and unique concern and are able to provide for each other's consummation, can each find his or her own fulfillment as a mature male and female. Indeed so many sexual relationships are frustrated and self-defeating because they provide nothing beyond genital functioning, with little or no interpersonal communication.

Mature sexual fulfillment provides the most intense esthetic experience and greatest intimacy of interpersonal relationships only when the sex partners can invest each other with all the worth and significance, offering each other the maximum of concern and tenderness. It is just this attribution of worth and of concern to a specific person which marks the contrast between organic mating and a love relationship wherein the identity of the sex partner and the reciprocal desire for each other are crucial. This has been one of the persistent aspirations of our culture, to transform sex, the organic functional process of mating, into an interpersonal love relationship.

Here again it is being shown that the capacity for this kind of sex-love is largely dependent upon prior experience of intimacy, affection, tenderness, since denial of these experiences in infancy and childhood seems to handicap the adult in establishing a love relationship where close tactual contacts and surrender are involved.

III

All human inventions are capable of being distorted, misused, turned into instruments for destruction and self-defeat. Language, the unique possession of man, is an instrument for communication, but is often used to deceive and mislead not only others but ourselves.

Ideas through which man has been able to create his various cultures and advance human living likewise may mislead and often imprison man, as the history of ideas so clearly shows. Ideas may also become agents of destruction and of self-defeat. Only man, who lives by ideas, can develop the mental disorders we call psychoses, when his ideas become so confused and contradictory that no longer is he able to orient himself to the social-cultural world of his fellows.

Purposive striving for deferred goals and consummations, the capacity for self-inhibition and for self-direction, these crucial patterns of human living may become so distorted, as in neurosis, that the individual is continually self-defeated.

Social order as the group's design for peaceful group living may become a tyrannical, dominant scheme of coercive exploitation.

Tools that have enabled man to create his varied designs for living and to utilize the potentialities of nature for his basic needs and enjoyment may be used as weapons for violence and annihilation of others. Science, the continual search for order and meaning in the universe, may provide productive techniques, life-saving remedies and protection of human existence, or instruments for destruction. Science may offer new and promising ideas and conceptions for advancing culture or for undermining morale by revealing the invalidity of what people have long believed.

It is not that the world is essentially evil and full of error, or that man is basically wicked and prone to destruction, but rather that all man's ideas and inventions are two-edged swords, that he can and often does use harmfully as well as beneficently. It is just this possibility of use for good or for ill that presents the essentially human problems of ethics to each person and to every culture and social order. The misuse, abuse, and distortion of man's inventions are always expressions of individual personalities.

No clearer example of this can be found than in human relationships, especially those that are called love. Just because the loving relationship is of such paramount significance, the expression of man's greatest potentiality, it is like other human inventions subject to an amazing variety of distortions and confusions, conflicts and tragic self-defeats.

For generations we have stressed in our traditions the supreme importance of love and have attempted in various ways to define and explain what love means and involves. Each generation has been reared in these traditions and has grown up seeking this *summum bonum* of life.

Today we are beginning to recognize how some of the confusion and conflicts and self-deception arise from the very ambiguity and conflict in our traditions and from the stunting and warping of our personalities.

Our traditions are conflicting because they have emphasized conditional love, as we are now calling it—the love that is given only as a reward for conformity, as a means of coercion, as something that will be withheld or withdrawn unless the recipient is obedient and submissive.

Conditional love is what parents have often given to their children: "I won't love you if you do that"; "If you want me to love you, you will do as I tell you"; "If you love me, you will do as I say." The parent who does this exploits the child's acute need for love and affection, for trust and confidence in his parents, in order to make him obedient. This practice often is effective because the child is terrified by the prospect of losing parental love, but it may create a lifelong pattern of relationship to others in which genuine, unconditional love and trust in others becomes impossible.

Our traditions are also confusing because they have imposed upon parents the dual roles of loving and punishing the child, who is expected to accept not only the necessary deprivations and frustrations for living in a social order but also physical pain, sometimes brutal punishment, considered necessary to rear the child as a social being.

Under such conflicting treatment, the child's early capacity to love may be so warped that he can never wholly believe in and rely upon another person whom he may wish to love. The memory of those early betrayals by the mother persists and blocks him from giving his love generously and confidently to another or of accepting the love of another.

Our traditions have created doubt and conflicts over the nature of loving because they have told the parents that to love the child they must inflict pain and punish every childish impulse as expressions of his evil nature. Not believing in the child, indeed convinced by our traditional teaching that human nature is evil and that the child must be coerced into giving up his evil, wicked impulses, parents have relied, not upon love but upon force, painful punishment and humiliation, and at the same time have told the child they love him and expect the child to love them.

These traditional beliefs and patterns of parents have been reinforced and sanctioned by our ancient belief in a deity who likewise offered conditional love, demanding submission and obedience for being loved. Indeed, over the centuries parents have told their children, as they punished them, "Whom the Lord loveth, He chasteneth!"

With such traditions it is not difficult to see how the conception of loving a person has been distorted and confused and why parents find it so difficult to love their child benevolently, unconditionally, with confidence in his capacity to become a responsible self-directing personality. Indeed, as we are just beginning to realize, the denial of love, the painful, often terrorizing punishments and threats of future punishment that we have relied upon to rear children and youth are probably the major sources of our many human failures and conflicts.

Despite our long and continued reiteration of the statement, "Love little children," we still are reluctant to love them generously and unconditionally. In consequence, few children grow up having experienced loving of the kind that orients them wisely and productively to adult life and loving.

There are also our literary and dramatic traditions about love which have been perplexing and confusing. For centuries poets, dramatists, and novelists have portrayed the relationship of men and women in terms of love, but that love has been interpreted in many diverse ways.

These portrayals have delineated the intensity of feelings, the sometimes obsessive concern for another, the often exaggerated admiration and praise of each other, all the outward expressions of loving, but have usually given little insight into the personality of the lovers, little understanding of the dynamics of loving.

The language used in these portrayals has provided a marvelous vocabulary for lovers' endearments, which can be used with varying meanings and intentions, often with little or no genuine expression of loving. Indeed, when we remember the extraordinary refinement of the language of love and courtship, the subtleties of expression for the Court of Love, it is doubtful whether any other human relationship has been given a more varied and ingenious expression.

But this very richness of language has obscured the basic lack of understanding of the loving relationship and made it possible for individuals to represent, not what they individually believed and felt, but what was expected or seemed appropriate to the occasion or, alas, what would deceive and mislead another.

Another source of difficulty has been that love has often meant to possess—literally, to own and have rights (as the common law expresses conjugal rights and duties) in another person. Only recently have we begun to recognize how often, in the name of love, we have denied the basic dignity and personal freedom of not only women but also children and adolescents, whom we may try to control and possess.

Indeed, it is clear that under the designation of love and of loving an amazing variety of actions, feelings, and relationships, often exploitative and destructive, may be found operating among so-called normal persons. Among neurotics and individuals who are unstable and subject to various kinds of warped feelings, an even more bizarre array may be found, including the widespread relationships of abject dependency and of unconscionable exploitation that are often called love.

Each personality brings to all interpersonal relationships the idiomatic patterns and chronic feelings he or she has developed through previous life experience. How each person will love will be governed by his personality and in his loving or attempts to love each may exhibit peculiar warping, stunting, distortions, sensitivities, or anesthesia, and especially chronic feelings of his own. These are often wholly irrelevant to the other person.

If we want to understand the varied expressions of loving with all the confusions, conflicts, and often tragic outcomes we see or hear about, we must see loving as arising from personalities who are expressing their peculiar version of our traditions and their idiomatic "private worlds" in their interpersonal relationships, often using the vocabulary and the gestures of loving but incapable of exhibiting what loving requires.

What is also of significance is that as human personalities we fluctuate in our feelings toward others. As Thornton Wilder has said in his exquisite novel, *The Woman of Andros:* "We can only be said to be alive when our hearts are conscious of our treasures, for we are not strong enough to love all the time." We cannot love all the time, and we may continue as adults to alternate between loving and hating the same person as we did in early childhood.

Indeed, nothing is more dramatic than the conversion of "love" that has been rejected into hostility.

We are, with few exceptions, continually engrossed in the play of human relationships where we seek to gain the recognition and if possible the admiration of others, as we attempt to invest others with the meanings that are significant for our "private worlds." Thus, we tend to see others as lovable or non-lovable and to seek the attention and response of those we consider lovable.

Often, however, the one we select to love is not responsive to our approach and all our efforts are of no avail. Some will then seek another person to love, but some will continue to hope that by further effort they can win the desired person's response. It cannot be overemphasized that, except for those who have been stunted or distorted, everyone is seeking to love and to be loved, since only in loving can we realize our humanness and live as personalities.

What is of tragic significance is that so many, many adults spend their whole adult lives in pursuing power, prestige, authority—all the outward signs and symbols of importance and significance—as substitutes for the loving they have failed to receive or could not give.

IV

Loving is indeed one of our most precious human potentialities, and the number and variety of conflicts and self-defeats involved in our attempts to love are further evidence of the crucial role of loving in human living.

To love another productively so that the loving is beneficent to both the beloved and the lover, is an essential human fulfillment that unfortunately most of us rarely if ever attain. Just as our lives are so frequently wrecked and our personalities distorted by the stunting and warping of sex, so the denial of loving imposes upon us intense frustration of our capacities for living fully and productively.

The far-reaching consequences of these unnecessary deprivations and frustrations for our culture and our social order, indeed for the world, are becoming ever clearer. We cannot attain our aspirations toward social order or develop a peaceful, orderly, and humanly desirable world community except by developing personalities who are capable of loving—loving and respecting themselves and also loving others.

The inability to love and to live fully and productively, with all the varied expressions of "man's inhumanity to man," are not fixed, unchangeable aspects of human nature but products of our traditions and our child-rearing and education that we can and must alter.

One does not need to be a Utopian dreamer to look forward to a world in which man's persistent aspirations may be increasingly realized, since their attainment is within our grasp as soon as we learn to utilize the potentialities of human nature that are now being wasted and tragically distorted. This calls for no magic formula but only the full acceptance and translation in practice of our enduring goals—human dignity, the dignity of man, woman, and child, beginning at birth.

Only through loving a person can we accord him the dignity he must have and feel to realize his potentialities and enable him to accord worth and dignity to others. The crucial test we must apply to all our traditions, including our religious traditions, is whether or not they provide that which will strengthen the personality, encourage the capacity for generous, unconditional love, and give the individual a belief in his own intrinsic worth and dignity, capable of living and loving fully and productively as a human being.

Maternal Love

Leon J. Saul, M.D.

Maternal Love

Leon J. Saul, M.D.

Love is a biological drive, or a combination of drives, which is not limited to human beings. There is a kernel of biological truth in the story of the suckling of Romulus and Remus by a she-wolf. My female boxer, the gift of friends some years ago, has suckled two litters of kittens and treated them like her own offspring.

This boxer is in her soul a lap dog, for she was much loved during the first year of her life and raised mostly within a home. But when she had her puppies she took to the fields and became a doughty hunter, bringing home rabbit after rabbit for her young, watching them and playing with them with endless patience and, of course, standing ready to defend them to the death against any danger.

Our cat delighted us with the same behavior. Previously content to do little more than lie in the sun, after the arrival of her kittens she took to the fields and woods and came back with small rodents as tidbits for her litter.

The birds, of course, provide us with such models of parental behavior as we humans can hardly hope to achieve. Have you ever watched for weeks and months a pair of phoebes, for example, building and repairing their nest and incessantly active in dropping food into the insatiable mouths of their chicks? The energy output is enormous and it is all devoted to other beings who will shortly grow up and leave the nest just as the young do in every species. Here there is no question of the young being raised in order to satisfy the parents' ambitions or to support them in their old age. This is love in the purest sense because it is productive, responsible, giving activity devoted to these other creatures for their own sake and without thought of return. This is the essence of "true love."

Wolves also provide examples which are probably beyond our human powers. For the wolves are not only excellent parents but apparently also are able to love devotedly and to get on harmoniously with their in-laws.

II

This devotion of the mother to the young is probably the model for loving, not only in human beings but biologically throughout the animal kingdom. Of course it has its deviations and aberrations and its examples of parents' mistreating and eating their offspring. But insofar as love can be pure and true, this appears to be it.

The father, as compared with the mother, is as one removed from the child. He does not bear it or suckle it, he does not have the mother's intimacy of contact with it. (There are, however, always variations and exceptions—for example it is the father sea-horse who takes over the baby sea-horses and carries them in a pouch similar to the pouch of kangaroos.) Yet the father's love for the young can also be powerful; and he comes to it in part through providing for and protecting his mate and her offspring. Thus his activities even in society represent the output of energies devoted to the rearing of the young. It has been suggested that the creativity of men in the arts and sciences has been so much greater than that of women because this productivity represents the energies which the women put into the bearing and rearing of children.

In any event, and to whatever extent paternal love follows the model of maternal love, the mother's love for her child is probably the purest example and model of what true love is. Moreover, it is itself one of the central goals, if not the central goal, of the man's love for the woman, i.e. to make a home for the production and rearing of young. Such love is by no means confined to human beings, since other mammals and birds mate for long periods and even for life. In this, many of them have better records of stable marriages than do human beings.

III

The love of the mother for her child is not only a model for love but for maturity. The mother and her young, in humans and in other species, represent the essence of maturity and immaturity respectively.

The offspring started life as a single cell. While within the womb it was completely parasitic. At birth it has to learn suddenly at least to breathe for itself and soon thereafter has to learn to swallow and take in food for itself. Gradually it gains the use of its senses, powers of locomotion; gradually it comes to be less utterly dependent upon the mother.

The mother represents the complement of this. The more parasitic the infant, the more giving must be the mother; the more helpless the child, the more protective must be the parent. The child sucks up energies, for its goal is its own growth and development. The mother pours out energies, for her goal is now to assure the best development of her offspring—not for any tangible return, not to fulfill her ambitions, not to support her, not for personal gain, but for the children's own sakes. To see them grow into lusty adulthood, able to be independent, to mate, to make their own way, and to rear healthy wholesome offspring of their own—this is the essential of true maternal love and the pattern for true paternal love also.

IV

This unselfish love of the mother for her child is also at the bottom of those feelings between human beings which make society possible. Human beings are not the only creatures to form societies. In fact almost all species do. One need think only of schools of fish, packs of wolves, hives of bees, flocks of birds. Only the exceptional species is not social. What holds these species in societies is not yet well known. No doubt it is a combination of many motives; but one powerful motive, as is evident from the study of human beings, lies in this capacity for love, which we see epitomized in the mother's relationship to the child.

V

"Love thy neighbor" is an ideal of Western culture, an ideal which is, as we all know to our sadness, only partially achieved. Many people try to love but cannot. And when we come to examine with great care why an individual is not able to love, we discover invariably that it is because he himself was not properly loved during the formative years of his childhood, that is, from conception to the age of six, seven, or eight. Perhaps he was not loved at all, perhaps he was loved not wisely but too well, but always something was wrong in the attitudes and feelings of the parents toward him during his tenderest years, and the parent who is closest to him is usually the mother. Often, of course, it is not the mother but the father who is to blame, which recalls the quip: "What is the best thing father can do for his children?" To which the answer is, "Love mother."

VI

If the child has not been loved with truly selfless interest in its own well-being and development, then, because of mistreatment, it develops reactions of resentment, rage, and hostility. These appear in disorders of behavior, in depressions, in feelings of persecution, in headaches, in derangements of the stomach, heart, and other organs. Indeed the functional neuroses and psychoses represent, as Freud said years ago, failures in the development of the ability to love. The failure of this development means that there are inner irritants—inner feelings of rejection, for example, or of being dominated—feelings of being in some way mistreated.

These inner threats and irritants in turn generate hatred; and this hostility and vengefulness appear not only in the form of neurotic, psychotic, and psychosomatic symptoms but also in behavior in life. Thereby it underlies frank criminality and white-collar criminality, and at bottom it is the grass-roots cause of war. A few evil individuals could not rise to power and lead a great nation into war if there were not a great deal of hostility throughout the population ready to be channeled by such leaders into open violence.

VII

To rear children is not easy. They must be domesticated to civilized social living, but this can very definitely be accomplished without ruining their emotional relationships with their parents.

The greatest single influence in their lives will be that of their mother, who during the earliest years is the one closest to them. If this love is pure, then the core of the child's personality will be sound and it will be strong to withstand the onslaught of life.

And this unselfish love of the mother toward her child should be emblazoned for us as a model of mature attitudes and behavior. From the picture of mother and child one can see what is mature and what is infantile; one can see the child's egocentric, parasitic "demandingness" and the mother's mature capacity for meeting the needs of the still weak and helpless creature.

The evils and suffering of mankind are the results of improper child-rearing, which foredooms the children to becoming insufficiently mature mothers and fathers.

But the voice of reason is powerful and persistent. As mankind gradually learns, becomes conscious of, and appreciates the significance of emotional maturity and of what goes into the development of this capacity to love, it will move nearer to these goals, and thereby further away from the results of impaired maturity and capacity to love, namely, neurosis, psychosis, criminality, disease, and war. It will move toward development and adaptation, toward strength, stability, cooperation.

The model is the mother's love for her child. Truly, the hand that rocks the cradle rules the world.

Love in Healthy People

A. H. Maslow

Love in Healthy People[*]

A. H. Maslow

(BRANDEIS UNIVERSITY)

It is amazing how little the empirical sciences have to offer on the subject of love. Particularly strange is the silence of the psychologists, for one might think this to be their particular obligation. Probably this is just another example of the besetting sin of the academicians, that they prefer to do what they are easily able rather than what they ought, like the kitchen helper I knew who opened every can in the hotel one day because he was so *very* good at opening cans.

Sometimes this is merely sad or irritating, as in the case of the textbooks of psychology and sociology, practically none of which treats the subject. The only real exceptions I have found are Symonds' *Dynamics of Human Adjustment* and various writings of Sorokin, of which the latest is a symposium, *Explorations in Altruistic Love and Behavior.*

More often the situation becomes completely ludicrous. One might reasonably expect that writers of serious treatises on the family, on marriage, and on sex should consider the subject of love to be a proper, even basic, part of their self-imposed task. But I must report that no single

---

[*] Numbers in brackets in the text refer to bibliographical references at the end of this chapter.

one of the volumes on these subjects available in the library where I work has any serious mention of the subject. More often, the word "love" is not even indexed.

I must confess that I understand this better now that I have undertaken the task myself. It is an extraordinarily difficult subject to handle in any tradition. And it is triply so in the scientific tradition. It is as if we were at the most advanced position in no-man's-land, at a point where the conventional techniques of orthodox psychological science are of very little use.

And yet our duty is clear. We *must* understand love; we must be able to teach it, to create it, to predict it, or else the world is lost to hostility and to suspicion. [3] The importance of the goal lends worth and dignity even to such unreliable data as are herein offered. Furthermore they are, so far as I know, the only "data" available on the subject.

The principle upon which the research proceeded was simple enough, however difficult it turned out to be in practice. On the basis of the psychiatric and psychological knowledge now available, I tried to find actual cases of psychiatric health from among all the people I knew or had heard of or had read about. They turned out to be extremely rare. I was able to turn up only about five to forty, depending on the rigor of my criteria, and the inclusion of doubtful and insufficiently known people. This was supplemented by studies with college students. No single one of about 4,000 students could be said to be truly self-actualizing, but the top one or two percent—in terms of healthiness—were selected out for testing and study. This research is still in progress.

This study is pre-scientific rather than scientific in the

ordinary sense. And yet the writer consoles himself with the fact that the shortcomings of this report arise out of intrinsic difficulties of the task and of the material rather than out of neglect, laziness, or carelessness. Probing and questioning are severely limited when one deals with people who a) are older than the questioner and b) have a much stronger sense of privacy than the average person. I learned early that I had to get my data indirectly rather than directly, subtly rather than bluntly, and that often it came in an equivocal form which I had to "interpret." I felt often like a detective working with circumstantial evidence rather than with eye-witness reports.

But all these difficulties become even more weighty when we deal with sex, love, and marriage. In this area my reticent subjects outdid themselves, and I must henceforth speak of "impressions" rather than of data.

The possibilities for projection of the investigator's own attitudes are obvious, and it is only fair to warn my readers about this source of unreliability. Various other difficulties of sampling and of statistics have been presented in my original report on self-actualizing (psychiatrically healthy) people. [22] The reader is referred to this paper for the background of the present report,[1] as well as for the possible criticisms of it.

1. A PRELIMINARY DESCRIPTION OF SOME CHARACTERISTICS OF LOVE BETWEEN THE SEXES

We shall mention first some of the better-known characteristics of love between the sexes and then proceed to

---

[1] Mimeographed copies of this paper are available for thirty-five cents postpaid from the Brandeis University Bookstore, Waltham, Mass. The journal in which it appeared is no longer in print.

the more special findings of our study of self-actualizing people. A very useful description to start with is available in Symonds' chapter on "Love and Self-Love" in his *Dynamics of Human Adjustment*. [34]

The core of the description of love must be subjective or phenomenological rather than objective or behavioral. No description, no words can ever communicate the full quality of the love experience to one who has himself never felt it. It consists primarily of a feeling of tenderness and affection with great enjoyment, happiness, and satisfaction in experiencing this feeling (if all is going well). There is a tendency to want to get closer, to come into more intimate contact, to touch and embrace the loved person, to yearn for him. This person furthermore is perceived in some desirable way, whether as beautiful, as good, or as attractive; in any case, there is pleasure in looking at and being with the loved one and distress in separation from him. Perhaps from this comes the tendency to focus attention upon the loved person, along with the tendency to forget other people, and to narrow perception in such a way that many things are not noticed. It is as if the loved person were in himself attractive, and *pulled* the attention and perception of the loving person. This feeling of pleasure in contact and in being with, shows itself also in the desire to be together with the loved one as much as possible in as many situations as possible: in work, in play, during esthetic and intellectual pursuits. There is often expressed a desire to share pleasant experiences with the loved person so that it is often reported that the pleasant experience is more pleasant because of the presence of the sweetheart.

Finally, of course, there is a special sexual arousal in the lover. This, in the typical instance, shows itself directly in genital changes. The beloved person seems to have a special power that nobody else in the world has to the same degree of producing erection and secretion in the partner, of arousing specific conscious sexual desire, and of producing the usual pricklings and tinglings that go with sexual arousal. And yet this is not essential, since love can be observed in people who are too old for sexual intercourse.

The desire for intimacy is not only physical but also psychological. It expresses itself frequently as a special taste for privacy for the pair. In addition to this, I have observed often the growth in a pair who love each other of a secret language, secret sexual words which other people can't understand, and of special tricks and gestures which only the lovers understand.

Quite characteristic is the feeling of generosity, of wanting to give and to please. The lover gets special pleasure from doing things for and making gifts to the loved one.

Very common is the desire for a fuller knowledge of one another, a yearning for a kind of psychological intimacy and psychological proximity and of being fully known to each other. Special delight in sharing secrets is common. Perhaps these are sub-examples which come under the broader heading of personality fusion of which we shall speak below.

A common example of the tendency to generosity and to do things for the one who is loved are the very common fantasies in which a person will imagine himself making great sacrifices for the sake of his sweetheart.

2. DROPPING OF DEFENSES IN SELF-ACTUALIZING
LOVE RELATIONSHIPS

Theodor Reik [27, p. 171] has defined one characteristic of love as the absence of anxiety. This is seen with exceptional clearness in healthy individuals. There is little question about the tendency to more and more complete spontaneity, the dropping of defenses, the dropping of roles, and of trying and striving in the relationship. As the relationship continues, there is a growing intimacy and honesty and self-expression, which at its height is a rare phenomenon. The report from these people is that with a beloved person it is possible to be oneself, to feel natural; "I can let my hair down." This honesty also includes allowing one's faults, weaknesses, and physical and psychological shortcomings to be freely seen by the partner.

There is much less tendency to put the best foot forward in the healthy love relationship. This goes so far as to make less likely the hiding even of physical defects of middle and old age, of false teeth, braces, girdles, and the like. There is much less maintenance of distance, mystery, and glamour, much less reserve and concealment and secrecy. This complete dropping of the guard definitely contradicts folk wisdom on the subject, not to mention some of the psychoanalytic theorists. For instance, Reik believes that being a good pal and being a good sweetheart are mutually exclusive and contradictory. Our data seem to indicate the contrary.

Our data definitely contradict also the age-old "intrinsic hostility between the sexes" theory. This hostility between the sexes, this suspicion of the opposite sex, this tendency to identify with one's own sex in an alliance against the other sex, even the very phrasing itself of "opposite sex" is found often enough in neurotic people and even in average citizens in our society, but it is definitely not found in self-actualizing people, at least with the resources for research that I had at my disposal.

Another finding that contradicts folk wisdom and also some of the more esoteric theorists on sexuality and love, for example, Guyon, is the definite finding that in self-actualizing people the love satisfactions and the sex satisfactions both improve with the age of the relationship. It is a very common report from these individuals that "sex is better than it used to be" and "seems to be improving all the time." It seems quite clear that even the strictly sensual and physical satisfactions are improved by familiarity with the partner rather than by novelty in healthy people. Of course, there is little doubt that novelty in the sexual partner is very exciting and attractive, especially for definitely neurotic people, but our data make it very unwise to make any generalization about this, and certainly not for self-actualizing people.

We may sum up this characteristic of self-actualizing love in the generalization that healthy love is in part an absence of defenses, that is to say, an increase in spontaneity and in honesty. The healthy love relationship tends to make it possible for two people to be spontaneous, to know each other and still to love each other. Of course, this implies that as one gets to know another person more and more intimately and profoundly, one will like what one sees. If the partner is profoundly "bad" rather than "good," then increasing familiarity will produce not increasing preference but increasing antagonism and revulsion. This reminds me of a finding that I made in a little study of the effects of familiarization on paintings. My finding was that "good" paintings become more and more preferred and enjoyed with increasing familiarization, but that "bad" paintings become less and less preferred. The difficulty of deciding at that time on some objective criterion of "good" and "bad" in paintings was so great that I preferred not to publish the finding. But if I may be permitted this amount of subjectivism, then I will say that the "better" people are, the more they will be loved with greater familiarity; the "worse" people are (by my standards) then the *less* they will be liked as familiarity increases.

One of the deepest satisfactions coming from the healthy love relationship reported by my subjects is that such a relationship permits the greatest spontaneity, the greatest naturalness, the greatest dropping of defenses and protection against threat. In such a relationship it is not necessary to be guarded, to conceal, to try to impress, to feel tense, to watch one's words or actions, to suppress or repress. My people report that they can be themselves without feeling that there are demands or expectations upon them; they can feel psychologically (as well as physically) naked and still feel loved and wanted and secure.

Rogers has described this well. [28, p. 159] " 'Loved' has here perhaps its deepest and most general meaning —that of being deeply understood and deeply accepted. . . . We can love a person only to the extent that we are not threatened by him; we can love only if his reactions to us, or to those things which affect us, are understandable to us. . . . Thus, if a person is hostile toward me, and I can see nothing in him at the moment except the hostility,

I am quite sure that I will react in a defensive way to the hostility."

Menninger [24] describes the reverse side of the coin. "Love is impaired less by the feeling that we are not appreciated than by a dread, more or less dimly felt by everyone, lest others see through our masks, the masks of repression that have been forced upon us by convention and culture. It is this that leads us to shun intimacy, to maintain friendships on a superficial level, to underestimate and fail to appreciate others lest they come to appreciate us too well."

3. THE ABILITY TO LOVE AND TO BE LOVED

My subjects were loved and were loving and are loved and are loving. In practically all (not quite all) my subjects where data were available, this tended to point to the conclusion that (all other things being equal) psychological health comes from being loved rather than from being deprived of love. [19, 22] Granted that the ascetic path is a possible one, and that frustration has some good effects; yet basic need-gratification seems to be much more the usual precursor or *Anlage* of health. This seems to be true not only for being loved but for loving as well. (That *other* requirements are also necessary is proven by the psychopathic personality, especially as exemplified by Levy's [18] indulged psychopath.)

It is also true of our self-actualizing people that they *now* love and are loved. For certain reasons it had better be said that they have the power to love and the ability to *be* loved. (Even though this may sound like a repetition of the sentence before, it really is not.) These are clinically observed facts, and are quite public and easily repeatable.

Menninger [24] makes the very acute statement that human beings really *do* want to love each other but just don't know how to go about it. This is much less true for healthy people. *They* at least know how to love, and can do so freely and easily and naturally and without getting wound up in conflicts or threats or inhibitions.

However, my subjects used the word "love" warily and with circumspection. They applied it only to a few rather than to many, tending to distinguish sharply between loving someone and liking him or being friendly or benevolent or brotherly. It describes for them an intense feeling, not a mild or disinterested one.

4. SEXUALITY IN SELF-ACTUALIZING LOVE

We can learn a very great deal from the peculiar and complex nature of sex in the love-life of self-actualizing people. It is by no means a simple story; there are many interwoven threads. On the whole, however, their sex life is characteristic and can be described in such a way as to make possible various conclusions, both positive and negative, about the nature of sex as well as about the nature of love.

For one thing it can be reported that sex and love can be and most often are very perfectly fused with each other in healthy people. While it is perfectly true that these are separable concepts, and while no purpose would be served in confusing them with each other unnecessarily [27, 33], still it must be reported that in the life of healthy people, they tend to become completely joined and merged with each other. As a matter of fact we may also say that they become less separable and less separate from each other in the lives of the people we have studied. We cannot go so far as some who say that any person who is capable of having sexual pleasure where there is no love must be a sick man. But we can certainly go in this direction. It is certainly fair to say that self-actualizing men and women tend on the whole not to seek sex for its own sake, or to be satisfied with it alone when it comes. I am not sure that my data permit me to say that they would rather not have sex at all if it came without affection, but I am quite sure that I have many instances in which for the time being at least sex was given up or rejected because it came without love and affection.

Another finding already reported [22] is the very strong impression that the sexual pleasures are found in their most intense and ecstatic perfection in self-actualizing people. If love is a yearning for the perfect and for complete fusion, then the orgasm as sometimes reported by self-actualizing people becomes the attainment of it. Experiences described in reports that I have obtained have indeed been at so great a level of intensity that I felt it justifiable to record them as "mystic experiences." Such phrases as "too big to assimilate," "too good to be true," "too good to last," etc., have been coupled with reports of being swept away completely by forces beyond control. This combination of very perfect and intense sexuality along with other characteristics to be reported produces several seeming paradoxes which I now wish to discuss.[2]

[2] Schwarz, Oswald, *The Psychology of Sex*, Penguin Books, Harmondsworth, Middlesex, 1951, p. 21: "Although totally different in nature, sexual impulse and love are dependent on, and complementary to, each other. *In a perfect, fully mature human being only this inseparable fusion of sexual impulse and love exists.* This is the

In self-actualizing people the orgasm is simultaneously more important and less important than in average people. It is often a profound and almost mystical experience, and yet the absence of sexuality is more easily tolerated by these people. This is not a paradox or a contradiction. It follows from dynamic motivation theory. Living at a higher need level makes the lower needs and their frustrations and satisfactions less important, less central, more easily neglected. But it also makes them more wholeheartedly enjoyed when gratified. [23]

An excellent parallel may be made between this and the attitude of these people toward food. Food is simultaneously enjoyed and yet regarded as relatively unimportant in the total scheme of life by self-actualizing people. When they do enjoy it, they can enjoy it whole-heartedly and without the slightest tainting with bad attitudes toward animality and the like. And yet ordinarily feeding oneself takes a relatively unimportant place in the total picture. These people do not *need* sensuality; they simply enjoy it when it occurs.

Certainly also food takes a relatively unimportant place in the philosophy of Utopia, in Heaven, in the good life, in the philosophy of values and ethics. It is something basic, to be taken for granted, to be used as a foundation stone upon which higher things are built. These people are very ready to recognize that the higher things cannot be built until the lower ones are built, but once these lower needs are satisfied, they recede from consciousness, and there is little preoccupation with them.

---

fundamental principle of any psychology of sex. If there be anyone capable of experiencing the purely physical gratification of sex, he is stigmatized as sexually subnormal (immature or otherwise)."

The same seems to be true for sex. Sex can be, as I said, wholeheartedly enjoyed, enjoyed far beyond the possibility of the average person, even at the same time that it does not play any central role in the philosophy of life. It is something to be enjoyed, something to be taken for granted, something to build upon, something that is very basically important like water or food, and which can be enjoyed as much as these; but gratification should be taken for granted. I think such an attitude as this resolves the apparent paradox in the self-actualizing person's simultaneously enjoying sex so much more intensely than the average person, yet at the same time considering it so much less important in the total frame of reference.

It should be stressed that from this same complex attitude toward sex arises the fact that the orgasm may bring on mystical experiences, and yet at other times may be taken rather lightly. This is to say that the sexual pleasure of self-actualizing people may be very intense or not intense at all. This conflicts with the romantic attitude that "love is a divine rapture, a transport, a mystic experience." It is true that it may be also a delicate pleasure rather than an intense one, a gay and light-hearted, playful sort of thing rather than a serious and profound experience or even a neutral duty. These people do not always live on the heights—they may live at a more average level of intensity, and lightly and mildly enjoy sex as a titillating, pleasant, playful, enjoyable, tickling kind of experience instead of a plumbing of the most intense depths of ecstatic emotionality. This is especially true when the subjects are relatively fatigued. Under such circumstances, the lighter kind of sex may take place.

Self-actualizing love shows many of the characteristics

of self-actualization in general. For instance, one characteristic is that it is based on a healthy acceptance of the self and of others. So much can be accepted by these people that others would not accept. For example, in spite of the fact that these people are relatively more monogamous than the average, and relatively less driven to love affairs outside the marriage, yet they are much more free than the average to admit to the fact of sexual attraction to others. My impression is that there tends to be a rather easy relationship with the opposite sex, along with casual acceptance of the phenomenon of being attracted to other people, at the same time that these individuals do rather less about this attraction than other people. Also it seems to me that their talk about sex is considerably more free and casual and unconventional than the average. Now what this sums up to is an acceptance of the facts of life, which, going along with the more intense and profound and satisfying love relationship, seems to make it less *necessary* to seek for compensatory or neurotic sex affairs outside the marriage. This is an interesting instance in which acceptance and behavior do not correlate. The easier acceptance of the facts of sexuality seems to make it easier rather than harder to be relatively monogamous.

In one instance, where the woman had long since separated from her husband, whatever information I was able to get from her indicated that she went in for what would be called promiscuity. She had sexual affairs and was very definite about how she enjoyed them. This was a fifty-five-year-old woman. I was never able to get more details than her statements that she did have such affairs and that she enjoyed sex very much. There was no slight element of guilt or anxiety or of the feeling of doing anything wrong in her conversation about this matter. Apparently the tendency to monogamy is not the same as the tendency to chastity, or a rejection of sexuality. It is just that the more profoundly satisfying the love relationship, the less necessity there is for all sorts of compulsions for sex affairs with people other than the wife or husband.

Of course, this acceptance of sexuality is also a main basis for the intensity of enjoyment of sexuality which I find in self-actualizing people. Another characteristic I found of love in healthy people is that they made no really sharp differentiation between the roles and personalities of the two sexes. That is, they did not assume that the female was passive and the male active, whether in sex or love or anything else. These people were all so certain of their maleness or femaleness that they did not mind taking on some of the cultural aspects of the opposite sex role. It was especially noteworthy that they could be both active and passive lovers and this was clearest in the sexual act and in physical love-making. Kissing and being kissed, being above or below in the sexual act, taking the initiative, being quiet and receiving love, teasing and being teased—these were all found in both sexes. The report indicated that both were enjoyed at different times. It was considered to be a shortcoming to be limited to just active love-making or passive love-making. Both have their particular pleasures for self-actualizing people.

This can go pretty far, almost to the point of reminding us of sadism and masochism. There can be a joy in being used, in subjection and passivity, even in accepting pain, in being exploited. Also, there can be an active and positive pleasure in squeezing and hugging and biting and in being violent and even in inflicting and receiving pain, so long as this does not get out of bounds.

Here again we have an instance of the way in which common dichotomies are so often resolved in self-actualization, appearing to be valid dichotomies only because people are not healthy enough.

This agrees with D'Arcy's [6] thesis that erotic and agapean love are basically different but merge in the best people. He speaks about two kinds of love which are ultimately masculine or feminine, active or passive, self-centered or self-effacing, and it is true that in the general run of the public these seem to contrast and be at opposite poles. However, it is different in healthy people. In these individuals the dichotomies are resolved, and the individual becomes both active and passive, both selfish and unselfish, both masculine and feminine, both self-interested and self-effacing. D'Arcy acknowledges that this occurs with extreme rarity.

One negative conclusion that our data, limited though they are, permit us to make with considerable confidence is that the Freudian tendency to derive love from sex or to identify them is a bad mistake.[3] Of course Freud is not alone in this error—it is shared by many less thoughtful citizens—but he may be taken as its most influential ex-

[3] Balint, M., "On Genital Love," *International Journal of Psychoanalysis*, 1948, 29, 34-40: "If one reads the psychoanalytical literature for references to genital love, to one's surprise two striking facts emerge: (a) much less has been written on genital love than on pre-genital love; (b) almost everything that has been written on genital love is negative." See also Balint, M., "The Final Goal of Psychoanalytic Treatment," *International Journal of Psychoanalysis*, 1936, 17, 206-216, p. 206.

ponent in Western civilization. There are traces here and there in Freud's writings that he had different thoughts about the matter occasionally. Once, for example, he spoke about the child's feeling for the mother as deriving from the "self-preservation" instincts, i. e., a kind of feeling akin to gratitude for being fed and cared for: "It [affection] springs from the very earliest years of childhood, and was formed on the foundation provided by the interests of the self-preservation instinct." [9, p. 204] In another place he interprets it as reaction formation [p. 252]; again, as the "mental side of the sexual impulse." [p. 259]

On the whole, however, the most widely accepted of the various theories put forth by Freud is the following: Tenderness is "aim-inhibited sexuality." [4] That is, to put it very bluntly, it is deflected and disguised sexuality. When we are forbidden to fulfill the sexual "aim" of coupling, and when we keep on wanting to and don't dare admit to ourselves that we are, then the compromise product is tenderness and affection. Contrariwise, whenever we meet with tenderness and affection we have no Freudian recourse but to regard this as "aim-inhibited" sexuality. Another deduction from this premise that seems unavoidable

[4] Freud, Sigmund, *Civilization and Its Discontents:* "These people make themselves independent of their object's acquiescence by transferring the main value from the fact of being loved to their own act of loving; they protect themselves against loss of it by attaching their love not to individual objects but to all men equally, and they avoid the uncertainties and disappointments of genital love by turning away from its sexual aim and modifying the instinct into an impulse with an *inhibited aim*. The state which they induce in themselves by this process—an unchangeable, undeviating, tender attitude —has little superficial likeness to the stormy vicissitudes of genital love, from which it is nevertheless derived."

is that if sex were never inhibited, and if everyone could couple with anyone else, then there would be no tender love. Incest taboos and repression—these are what breed love. For other views see our bibliography. [4, 5, 17, 29]

Another kind of love discussed by the Freudians is "genital love," frequently defined with exclusive emphasis on "genital" and without any reference to "love." For instance, it is often defined as the power to be potent, to have a good orgasm, to have this orgasm from penile-vaginal coupling without the *necessity* of recourse to clitoris, anus, sadism, masochism, etc. The best statement in the Freudian tradition I have been able to find is the one by Michael Balint.[5]

[5] Balint, M., "On Genital Love," *International Journal of Psychoanalysis,* 1948, 29, 34-40: "To avoid this pitfall [emphasis on negative qualities] let us examine an ideal case of such postambivalent genital love that has no traces of ambivalency and in addition no traces of pre-genital object relationship; (a) there should be no greediness, no insatiability, no wish to devour the object, to deny it any independent existence, i.e., there should be no oral features; (b) there should be no wish to hurt, to humiliate, to boss, to dominate the object, etc., i.e., no sadistic features; (c) there should be no wish to defile the partner, to despise him (her) for his (her) sexual desires and pleasures. There should be no danger of being disgusted by the partner or being attracted only by some unpleasant features of him, etc., and there should be no remnants of anal traits; (d) there should be no compulsion to boast about the possession of a penis, no fear of the partner's sexual organs, no fear for one's own sexual organs, no envy of the male or female genitalia, no feeling of being incomplete or of having a faulty sexual organ, or of the partner having a faulty one, etc. There should be no trace of the phallic phase or of the castration complex. . . . What is then 'genital love' apart from the absence of all the enumerated pregenital traits? Well, we love our partner (1) because he or she can satisfy us; (2) because we can satisfy him or her; because we can experience a full orgasm together

How tenderness is involved in genital love remains a mystery, for in sexual intercourse there is, of course, no inhibition of the sexual aim (it *is* the sexual aim). Nothing has been said by Freud of aim-*gratified* sexuality. If tenderness is found in genital love, then some source other than aim-inhibition must be found, a non-sexual source, it would seem. Suttie's analysis [33] very effectively reveals the weaknesses of this position. So also do those of Reik [27], Fromm [13, 14], DeForest [7], and others in the revisionist-Freudian tradition. Adler [2] in 1908 affirmed that the need for affection was not derived from sex.

5. CARE, RESPONSIBILITY, THE POOLING OF NEEDS

One important aspect of a good love relationship is what may be called need-identification or the pooling of the hierarchies of basic needs in two persons into a single hierarchy. The effect of this is that one person feels another's needs as if they were his own and for that matter also feels his own needs to some extent as if they belonged to the

---

nearly or quite simultaneously. . . . Genital satisfaction is apparently only a necessary and not a sufficient condition of genital love. What we have learned is that genital love is much more than gratitude for or contentment about the partner being available for genital satisfaction. Further that it does not make any difference whether this gratitude or contentment is onesided or mutual. What is this? We find in addition to the genital satisfaction in a true love relation (1) idealization; (2) tenderness; (3) a special form of identification. To sum up: Genital love in man is really a misnomer. . . . What we call genital love is a fusion of disagreeing elements, genital satisfaction and pregenital tenderness . . . the reward for fearing the strain of this fusion is the possibility of regressing periodically for some happy moments to a really infantile stage of *no* reality testing. . . ."

other. An ego now expands to cover two people, and to some extent the two people have become for psychological purposes a single unit, a single person, a single ego.

This principle, probably first presented in technical form by Alfred Adler [2,8,35], has been very well phrased by Erich Fromm [14], particularly in his book *Man for Himself,* in which love is defined as follows: "Love, in principle, is indivisible as far as the connection between 'objects' and one's own self is concerned. Genuine love is an expression of productiveness and implies care, respect, responsibility, and knowledge. It is not an 'affect' in the sense of being affected by somebody, but an active striving for the growth and happiness of the loved person, rooted in one's own capacity to love" (pp. 129-130).

Schlick [30, p. 186] has also phrased this well: "The social impulses are those dispositions of a person by virtue of which the idea of a pleasant or unpleasant state of *another* person is itself a pleasant or unpleasant experience (also the mere perception of another creature, his presence alone, can by virtue of such an impulse, elicit feelings of pleasure). The natural effect of these inclinations is that their bearer establishes the joyful states of others as ends of his conduct. And, upon realization of these ends he enjoys the resultant pleasure; for not only the idea, but also the actual perception of the expression of joy pleases him."

The ordinary way in which this need-identification shows itself to the eyes of the world is in terms of taking on responsibility, of care, of concern for another person. The loving husband can get as much pleasure from his wife's pleasure as he can from his own. The loving mother would much rather cough herself than hear her child cough, and as a matter of fact would willingly take on to her own shoulders the disease of her child, since it would be less painful for her to have it than to see and hear her child have it. A good example of this is seen in the differential reactions in good marriages and bad marriages to illness and the consequently necessary nursing. An illness in the good couple is an illness of the couple rather than a misfortune of one of the pair. Equal responsibility is automatically taken, and it is as if they were both simultaneously struck. The primitive communism of the loving family shows itself in this way and not only in the sharing of food or of money. It is here that one sees at its best and purest the exemplification of the principle: from each according to his abilities and to each according to his needs. The only modification that is here necessary is that the needs of the other person *are* the needs of the lover.

If the relationship is a very good one, then the sick or weak one can throw himself upon the nursing care and the protectiveness of the loving partner with the same abandonment and lack of threat and lack of self-consciousness that a child shows in falling asleep in his parent's arms. It is often enough observed in less healthy couples that illness makes a strain in the couple. For the strong man whose masculinity is practically identified with physical strength, illness and weakness is a catastrophe and so is it also for his wife if she has defined masculinity in the same way. For the woman who defines femininity in terms of physical attractiveness of the beauty contest style, then illness or weakness or anything else that lessens her physical attractiveness is for her a tragedy, and for the man as well if he defines femininity in the same way. Our healthy people are almost completely exempted from this mistake.

If we remember that human beings are in the last analysis isolated from each other and encapsulated, each one in his own little shell, and if we agree that also in the last analysis people can never really know each other as they know themselves, then every intercourse between groups and individuals is like an effort of "two solitudes to protect, and touch and greet each other" (Rilke). Of all such efforts that we know anything about, the healthy love relationship is the most effective way of bridging the unbridgable gap between two separate human beings.

In the history of theorizing about love relations as well as about altruism, patriotism, etc., much has been said about the transcendence of the ego. An excellent modern discussion of this tendency at the technical level is afforded in a book by Angyal [1], in which he discusses various examples of a tendency to what he calls heteronomy, and which he contrasts with the tendency to autonomy, to independence, to individuality, and the like. More and more clinical and historical evidence accumulates to indicate that Angyal is right in demanding that some room be made in a systematic psychology for these various tendencies to go out beyond the limits of the ego. Furthermore, it seems quite clear that this need to go out beyond the limits of the ego may be a need in the same sense that we have needs for vitamins and minerals, i. e., that if the need is not satisfied, the person becomes sick in one way or another. I should say that the most satisfying and most complete example of ego transcendence, and certainly the most healthy from the point of view of avoiding illness of the character, is the throwing of oneself into a healthy love relationship.

6. FUN AND GAIETY IN THE HEALTHY LOVE RELATIONSHIP

The concepts of Erich Fromm and Alfred Adler which were mentioned above stress productiveness, care, responsibility. This is all very true, but Fromm, Adler, and the others who write in the same vein strangely omit one aspect of the healthy love relationship which was very clear in my subjects: namely, fun, merriment, gaiety. It is quite characteristic of self-actualizing people that they can enjoy themselves in love and in sex. Sex very frequently becomes a kind of a game in which laughter is quite as common as panting. The way in which Fromm and other serious thinkers on the subject have described the ideal love relationship is to make it into something of a task or a burden rather than a game or a pleasure. When Fromm [14, p. 110] says: "Love is the productive form of relatedness to others and to oneself. It implies responsibility, care, respect and knowledge, and the wish for the other person to grow and develop. It is the expression of intimacy between two human beings under the condition of the preservation of each other's integrity," it must be admitted that this sounds a little like a pact or a partnership of some kind, rather than a spontaneous sportiveness. It is not the welfare of the species, or the task of reproduction, or the future development of mankind that attracts people to each other. The sex life of healthy people, in spite of the fact that it frequently reaches great peaks of ecstasy, is nevertheless also easily compared to the games of children and puppies. It is cheerful, humorous, and playful. We shall point out in greater detail below that it is not primarily a striving, as Fromm implies; it is basically an enjoyment and a delight, which is another thing altogether.

7. ACCEPTANCE OF THE OTHER'S INDIVIDUALITY;
RESPECT FOR THE OTHER

All serious writers on the subject of ideal or healthy love have stressed the affirmation of the other's individuality, the eagerness for the growth of the other, the essential respect for his individuality and unique personality. This is confirmed very strongly by the observation of self-actualizing people, who have in unusual measure the rare ability to be pleased rather than threatened by the partner's triumphs. They do indeed respect their partners in a very profound and basic way which has many, many implications. As Overstreet says quite well [26, p.103], "The love of a person implies, not the possession of that person, but the affirmation of that person. It means granting him, gladly, the full right to his unique manhood."

Fromm's statement on the subject is also very impressive [13, p. 261]: "Love is the foremost component of such spontaneity; not love as the dissolution of the self in another person, but love as a spontaneous affirmation of others, as the union of the individual with others on the basis of the preservation of the individual himself." A most impressive example of this respect is the ungrudging pride of such a man in his wife's achievements, even where they outshine his. Another is the absence of jealousy.

This respect shows itself in many ways which, incidentally, had better be differentiated from the effects of the love relationship *per se*. Love and respect are separable, even though they often go together. It is possible to respect without loving, even at the self-actualizing level. I am not quite so sure that it is possible to love without respecting, but this too may be a possibility. Many of the characteristics that might be considered aspects or attributes of the love relationship are very frequently seen to be attributes of the respect relationship.

Respect for another person acknowledges him as an independent entity and as a separate and autonomous individual. The self-actualizing person will not casually use another or control him or disregard his wishes. He will allow the respected person a fundamental irreducible dignity, and will not unnecessarily humiliate him. This is true not only for inter-adult relationships but also in a self-actualizing person's relationship to children. It is possible for him, as for practically nobody else in our culture, to treat a child with real respect.

One amusing aspect of this respect relationship between the sexes is that it is very frequently interpreted in just the opposite way, i. e., as a lack of respect. For example, we know well that a good many of the so-called signs of respect for "ladies" are in fact hangovers from a non-respecting past, and possibly even at this time are unconscious representations of a deep unconscious contempt for women. Such cultural habits as standing up when a lady enters the room, giving a lady the chair, helping her with her coat, allowing her to go first through the door, giving her the best of everything and the first choice of everything—these all imply historically and dynamically the opinion that the woman is weak and incapable of taking care of herself, for these all imply protection, as for the weak and incapable. Generally, women who respect themselves strongly tend to dislike these signs of "respect," knowing full well that they may mean just the opposite. Self-actualizing men who tend really and basically to respect and to like women as partners, as equals, as pals, and as full human beings rather than as partial members of the species, are apt to be much more easy and free and familiar and "impolite" in the traditional sense. I have seen this make for trouble, and I have seen self-actualizing men accused of lack of "respect" for women.

8. LOVE AS END-EXPERIENCE; ADMIRATION; WONDER; AWE

The fact that love has many good effects does not mean that it is motivated by those effects or that people fall in love *in order* to achieve them. The love that is found in healthy people is much better described in terms of spontaneous admiration and of the kind of receptive and undemanding awe and enjoyment which we experience when struck by a fine painting. There is too much talk in the literature of rewards and purposes, of reinforcements and gratifications, and not nearly enough of what we may call the "end-experience" (as contrasted with the "means-experience") or "awe-before-the-beautiful."

Admiration and love in my subjects are most of the time *per se* undemanding of rewards and conducive to no purposes, "experienced," in Northrop's Eastern sense [25], concretely and richly, for their own sake, ideographically. [20]

Admiration asks for nothing and gets nothing. It is more passive than active and comes close to simple receiving in the naive-realistic sense. The awed perceiver does little or nothing to the experience; rather it does something to him. He watches and stares with the Innocent Eye, like a child who neither agrees nor disagrees, approves nor disapproves, but who, fascinated by the intrinsic attention-attracting quality of the experience, simply lets it come in and achieve its effects. The experience may be likened to the eager passivity with which we allow ourselves to be tumbled by waves just for the fun that's in it; or perhaps better, to the impersonal interest and awed unprojecting appreciation of the slowly changing sunset. There is little we can inject into a sunset. In this sense we do not project ourselves into the experience or attempt to shape it as we do with the Rorschach. Nor is it a signal or symbol for anything; we have not been rewarded or associated into admiring it. It has nothing to do with milk, or food, or other body needs. In the same way we can enjoy a painting without wanting to own it, a rosebush without wanting to pluck from it, a pretty baby without wanting to kidnap it, a bird without wanting to cage it, and so also can one person admire and enjoy another in a non-doing or non-getting way. Of course awe and admiration lie side by side with other tendencies that *do* involve individuals with each other; it is not the *only* tendency in the picture, but it is definitely part of it, especially in people who are less ego-involved.

Perhaps the most important implication of this observation is that we thereby contradict most theories of love, for most theorists assume that people are *driven* into loving another rather than *attracted* into it. Freud [12] speaks of aim-inhibited sexuality, Reik [27] speaks of aim-inhibited power, and many speak of dissatisfaction with the self forcing us to create a projected hallucination, an unreal (because overestimated) partner.

But it seems clear that healthy people fall in love the

way one reacts to one's first appreciative perception of great music—one is awed and overwhelmed by it and loves it. This is so even though there was no prior need to be overwhelmed by great music. Horney in a lecture has defined un-neurotic love in terms of regarding others as *per se,* as ends-in-themselves rather than as means-to-ends. The consequent reaction is to enjoy, to admire, to be delighted, to contemplate and appreciate, rather than to use. St. Bernard said it very aptly: "Love seeks no cause beyond itself and no limit; it is its own fruit, its own enjoyment. I love because I love; I love in order that I may love. . . ." [15]

Similar statements are available in abundance in the theological literature. [6] The effort to differentiate godly love from human love was often based on the assumption that disinterested admiration and altruistic love could be only a superhuman ability and not a natural human one. Of course, we must contradict this; human beings at their best, fully grown, show many *other* characteristics once thought, in an earlier era, to be supernatural prerogatives.

It is my opinion that these phenomena are best understood in the framework of certain theoretical considerations. I have presented these in previous papers. [19-23] In the first place, let us consider the differentiation between deficiency-motivation and growth-motivation (or better, growth-expression). I have suggested that self-actualizers can be defined as people who are no longer motivated by the needs for safety, belongingness, love, status, and self-respect because these needs *have already been satisfied.* Why then should a love-gratified person fall in love? Certainly not for the same reasons that motivate the love-deprived person, who falls in love because he needs and craves love, because he lacks it, and is impelled to make up this pathogenic deficiency.

Self-actualizers have no deficiencies to make up and must now be looked upon as freed for growth, maturation, development, in a word, for the fulfillment and actualization of their highest individual and species nature. What such people do emanates from growth and expresses it without striving. They love because they are loving persons, in the same way that they are kind, honest, natural, i.e., because it is their nature to be so spontaneously, as a strong man is strong without willing to be, as a rose emits perfume, or as a child is childish. Such epiphenomena are as little motivated as is physical growth or psychological maturation.

There is no trying, straining, or striving in the loving of the self-actualizer as there is in the loving of the average person. If we say that it is an aspect of Being as well as of Becoming, those who are familiar with the philosophical literature will understand.

9. DETACHMENT AND INDIVIDUALITY

A paradox seems to be created at first sight by the fact that self-actualizing people maintain a degree of individuality, of detachment and autonomy which seems at first glance to be incompatible with the kind of identification and love that I have been describing above. But this is only an apparent paradox. In fact the tendencies existing in the same man to detachment and to need-identification and to profound interrelationships with another person can all co-exist in healthy people. The fact is that self-actualizing people are simultaneously the most individualistic and the most altruistic and social and loving of all human beings. The fact that we have in our culture put these qualities at opposite ends of a single continuum is apparently a mistake that must now be corrected. These qualities go together and the dichotomy is resolved in self-actualizing people.

We find in our subjects a healthy selfishness, a great self-respect, a disinclination to make sacrifices without good reason.

What we see in the love relationship is a fusion of great ability to love and at the same time great respect for the other and great respect for one's self. This shows itself in the fact that these people cannot be said in the ordinary sense of the word to *need* each other as do ordinary lovers. They can be extremely close together and yet go apart quite easily. They do not cling to each other or have hooks or anchors of any kind. One has the definite feeling that they enjoy each other tremendously but would take philosophically a long separation or death. Throughout the most intense and ecstatic love affairs, these people remain themselves and remain ultimately masters of themselves as well, living by their own standards even though enjoying each other intensely.

Obviously, this finding, if confirmed, will necessitate a revision or at least an extension in the definition of ideal or healthy love in our culture. We have customarily defined it in terms of a complete merging of egos and a loss of separateness, a giving up of individuality rather than a strengthening of it. While this is true, the fact appears to be at this moment that the individuality is strengthened, that the ego is in one sense merged with another, but yet in another sense remains separate and strong as always. The two tendencies, to transcend individuality and to sharpen and strengthen it, must be seen as partners and not as contradictories.

10. THE GREATER TASTE AND PERCEPTIVENESS OF HEALTHY LOVERS

One of the most striking superiorities reported of self-actualizing people is their exceptional perceptiveness. They can perceive truth and reality far more efficiently than the average run of people, whether it is structured or unstructured, personal or non-personal.

This acuity manifests itself in the area of love-relations primarily in an excellent taste (or perceptiveness) in sexual and love partners. The close friends, husbands, and wives of our subjects make a far finer group of human beings than random sampling would dictate.

This is not to say that *all* the observed marriages and choices of sexual partner were at the self-actualizing level. Several mistakes can be reported, and although they can be to some extent explained away, they testify to the fact that our subjects are not perfect or omniscient. They have their vanities and their own special weaknesses. For example, at least one man of those I studied married more out of pity than out of equalitarian love. One married a woman much younger than himself, in the face of the inevitable problems. A measured statement would then stress that their taste in mates, while much better than average, is by no means perfect.

But even this is enough to contradict the generally held belief that love is blind or, in the more sophisticated versions of this mistake, that the lover necessarily overestimates his partner. It is quite clear that, though this probably is true for average people, it need not be true for healthy individuals. Indeed, there are even some indications that the perceptions of healthy people are *more* efficient, more acute when in love than when not. Love may make it possible to see qualities in the loved person of which others are completely oblivious.[6] It is easy enough to make this mistake because healthy people can fall in love with people whom others would not love for very definite "faults." However, this love is not blind to the faults; it simply overlooks these perceived faults, or else does not regard them as shortcomings. Thus physical imperfections, as well as economic, educational, and social shortcomings, are far less important to healthy people than are character defects. As a consequence, it is easily possible for self-actualizing people to fall deeply in love with homely partners. This is called blindness by others, but it might much better be called good taste.

I have had the opportunity of watching the development of this "good taste" in several relatively healthy young college men and women. The more mature they became, the less attracted they were by such characteristics as "handsome," "good-looking," "good dancer," "nice breasts," "physically strong," "tall," "handsome body," "good necker," and the more they spoke of com-

[6] Schwarz, Oswald, *The Psychology of Sex*, Penguin Books, Harmondsworth, Middlesex, 1951: "It cannot be emphasized strongly enough that this miraculous capacity which love bestows on the lovers consists in the power to discover in the object of love virtues which it actually possesses but which are invisible to the uninspired; they are not invented by the lover, who decorates the beloved with illusory values: love is no self-deception." (pp. 100-101) "No doubt there is a strong emotional element in it but essentially love is a cognitive act, indeed the only way to grasp the innermost core of personality." (p. 20)

patibility, goodness, decency, good companionship, considerateness. In a few cases, it could actually be seen that they fell in love with individuals with characteristics considered specifically distasteful a few years before, e.g., hair on the body, too fat, not smart enough. In one young man, I have seen the number of potential sweethearts grow fewer year by year until, from being attracted to practically any one female, and with exclusions being solely on a physical basis (too fat, too tall), he could think of making love with only two girls from among all that he knew. These were now spoken of in characterological rather than physical terms.

I think research will show that this is more characteristic of increasing health than simply of increasing age.

Two other common theories are contradicted by our data. One is that opposites attract, and the other is that like marries like (homogamy). The facts of the matter are that in healthy people homogamy is the rule with respect to such character traits as honesty, sincerity, kindliness, and courage. In the more external and superficial characteristics, e.g., income, class status, education, religion, national background, appearance, the extent of homogamy seems to be significantly less than in average people. Self-actualizing people are not threatened by differences nor by strangeness. Indeed, they are rather intrigued than otherwise. They need familiar accents, clothes, food, customs, and ceremonies much less than do average people. [22]

As for opposites attracting, this is true for my subjects to the extent that I have seen honest admiration for skills and talents which they themselves do not possess. Such superiorities make a potential partner *more* rather than less attractive to my subjects, whether in man or in woman.

Finally, I wish to call attention to another implication of considerable importance. The last few pages amount to a resolution or denial of the age-old dichotomy between impulse and reason, between "head" and "heart." The people with whom my subjects fall in love are soundly selected by *either* cognitive or conative criteria. That is, they are *intuitively, sexually, impulsively* attracted to people who are right for them by cold, intellectual, clinical calculation. Their appetites agree with their judgments, and are synergetic rather than antagonistic, as they very frequently are in average people and neurotics.

This reminds us of Sorokin's efforts [32] to demonstrate that the true, the good, and the beautiful are positively interrelated. Our data seem to confirm Sorokin, but *only for healthy people*. With respect to neurotic people, we must remain circumspect on this question.

11. THE RESOLUTION OF DICHOTOMIES IN SELF-ACTUALIZATION

I cannot resist the temptation to underscore a theoretical conclusion to which I have come from the study of self-actualizing people. At several points in this paper —and in other papers as well—it was concluded that what had been considered polarities or dichotomies were so *only in unhealthy people*. This was so for selfishness-unselfishness, reason-instinct (or cognition-conation), individualism-social mindedness, animality-"soulfulness," kindness-ruthlessness, concrete-abstract, acceptance-rebellion, self-society, adjustment-maladjustment, detachment from others-identification with others, childlikeness-maturity, serious-humorous, democratic-aristocratic, moral-amoral, classical-romantic, Apollonian-Dionysian, introverted-extraverted, intense-casual, conventional-unconventional, mystic-realistic, active-passive, masculine-feminine, lust-love, and Eros-Agape.

Fully matured people seem to be so different from average citizens in *kind* as well as in degree that I have come to suspect that the two very different kinds of people will generate two very different psychologies. The psychology that we now teach, being based upon the study of crippled, immature, and unhealthy specimens, must be suspected of not being large enough to encompass healthy, fully grown specimens. The cripple-psychology, which is all we now have, must be integrated with, imbedded in, and encompassed by a larger, more inclusive, more universal science of psychology. Such a science must be based upon the study of healthy self actualizing people.

Bibliography

1. Angyal, A., *Foundations For a Science of Personality*, New York, Commonwealth Fund, 1941.
2. Ansbacher, H., A forthcoming book of readings from the works of Alfred Adler.
3. Ashley Montagu, M. F., *On Being Human*, New York, H. Schuman, 1950.
4. Balint, M., "On Genital Love," *International Journal of Psychoanalysis*, 1948, 29, 34-40.
5. Bergler, E., *Neurotic Counterfeit-Sex*, New York, Grune and Stratton, 1951.
6. D'Arcy, *The Mind and Heart of Love*, New York, Holt, 1947.
7. DeForest, I., "Love and Anger, the Two Activating Forces in Psychoanalytic Therapy," *Psychiatry*, 1944, 7, 15-29.
8. Dreikurs, R., *The Challenge of Marriage*, New York, Duell, Sloan and Pearce, 1946.

9. Freud, S., *Collected Papers*, Vol. II, London, Hogarth, 1925.
10. Freud, S., *General Introduction to Psychoanalysis*, New York, Garden City Publishing Co., 1920.
11. Freud, S., *Contributions to the Psychology of Love*, Papers XI, XII, XIII in *Collected Papers*, Vol. 4, 192-235, London, Hogarth, 1925.
12. Freud, S., *Civilization and Its Discontents*, New York, Cape and Smith, 1930.
13. Fromm, E., *Escape From Freedom*, New York, Farrar and Rinehart, 1941.
14. Fromm, E., *Man For Himself*, New York, Rinehart, 1947.
15. Huxley, A., *The Perennial Philosophy*, New York, Harper, 1945.
16. Iovetz-Tereshchenko, N., *Friendship—Love in Adolescence*, London, George Allen and Unwin, 1936.
17. Jekels, L., and Bergler, E., "Transference and Love," *Psychoanalytic Quarterly*, 1949, 18, 325-350.
18. Levy, D. M., "The Deprived and Indulged Forms of Psychopathic Personality," *American Journal of Orthopsychiatry*, 1951, 21, 250-254.
19. Maslow, A. H., "Some Theoretical Consequences of Basic Need-Gratification," *Journal of Personality*, 1948, 16, 402-416.
20. Maslow, A. H., "The Expressive Component of Behavior," *Psychological Review*, 1949, 56, 261-272.
21. Maslow, A. H., "Resistance to Acculturation," *Journal of Social Issues*, 1951, 7, 4, 26-29.
22. Maslow, A. H., "Self-Actualizing People; a Study in Psychological Health," *Personality*, 1950, 1, 11-34 (Symposium No. 1 on Values).
23. Maslow, A. H., "The Instinctoid Nature of Basic Needs," *Journal of Personality*, 1952.
24. Menninger, K., *Love against Hate*, London, Kegan Paul, Trench, Trubner, 1935.
25. Northrop, F. S. C., *The Meeting of East and West*, New York, Macmillan, 1946.
26. Overstreet, H., *The Mature Mind*, New York, W. W. Norton, 1949.
27. Reik, T., *The Psychology of Sex Relations*, New York, Farrar and Rinehart, 1945.
28. Rogers, C., *Client-Centered Therapy*, New York, Houghton Mifflin, 1951.
29. Saul, L., *Emotional Maturity*, Philadelphia, Lippincott, 1947.
30. Schlick, M., *Problems of Ethics*, New York, Prentice-Hall, 1939.
31. Schwarz, O., *The Psychology of Sex*, Penguin Books, 1951.
32. Sorokin, P. (Editor), *Explorations in Altruistic Love and Behavior*, Boston, Beacon Press, 1950.

33. Suttie, I., *The Origins of Love and Hate,* New York, Julian Press, 1952.
34. Symonds, P., *The Dynamics of Human Adjustment,* New York, Appleton-Century-Crofts, 1946.
35. Wexberg, E., *The Psychology of Sex,* New York, Farrar and Rinehart, 1931.

The Power
of Creative Love

◊◊◊◊◊◊◊◊◊◊◊◊◊◊◊◊◊◊◊◊◊◊◊◊◊◊

Pitirim A. Sorokin
and
Robert C. Hanson

The Power
of Creative Love

Pitirim A. Sorokin
and
Robert C. Hanson

1. PREVALENT VIEWS

In the atmosphere of our Sensate[1] culture we are prone to believe in the power of the struggle for existence, selfish interests, egoistic competition, hate, fighting instinct, sex-drive, instinct of death and destruction, all-powerful economic factors, in the power of rude coercion and of other negativistic forces. And we are highly skeptical in regard to the power of creative love, disinterested service, unprofitable sacrifice, mutual aid, the call of pure duty and other positive forces. The prevalent theories of evolution and progress, of the dynamic forces of history, of the dominant factors of human behavior, of the how and why of social processes—these theories unanimously stress the above-mentioned negativistic factors. They view them as the main "determinants" of historical events and of

[1] Cf. on Sensate culture and mentality, P. Sorokin, *Social and Cultural Dynamics* (New York, 1937-41), 4 vols.; P. Sorokin, *Crisis of Our Age* (New York, 1941); F. R. Cowell, *History, Civilization and Culture: An Introduction to the Historical and Social Philosophy of Pitirim A. Sorokin* (London, 1952); J. Maquet, *The Sociology of Knowledge* (Boston, 1951).

the individual life-courses. Marvism and the "economic interpretation of history"; Freudianism and its "libidinal-destructive" explanation of human behavior; "instinctivist," "behaviorist," and "psychosomatic" theories of personality and culture; Darwinistic and biological theories of the struggle for existence as the main factor of biological, mental, and moral evolution; even the prevalent motto of the Chambers of Commerce that "rivalry and competition made America great";[2] these and similar theories dominate contemporary sociology, economics, psychology, psychiatry, biology, anthropology, philosophy of history, political science, and other social and humanistic disciplines. These ideologies have an enormous appeal to the prevalent Sensate mind; are eagerly believed by Sensate man; and are considered by him as "the last word of modern science."

In contrast to that we emphatically disbelieve the power of love, sacrifice, friendship, cooperation, call of duty, unselfish search for truth, goodness, and beauty. These appear to us as something epiphenomenal and illusory. We call them by the terms: "rationalizations," "self-deceptions," "derivations," "beautifying ideologies," "opiate of the people's mind," "smoke-screens, "idealistic bosh," "unscientific delusions," etc. We are biased against all theories that try to prove the power of love and other positive forces in determining human behavior and personality; in influencing the course of biological, social, mental, and moral evolution; in affecting the direction of historical events; in shaping social institutions and culture.

[2] Cf. on these theories P. Sorokin, *Contemporary Sociological Theories* (New York, 1928).

This penchant to believe in the power of the negative forces and to disbelieve the influence of the positive energies has nothing to do with the scientific validity of both kinds of theories. It is mainly the result of the congeniality of the "debunking negativistic theories" with the negativistic character of the decaying Sensate culture and of the non-congeniality of the positive, "idealistic" theories with this Sensate culture. The negativistic theories are "the flesh of the flesh and the bone of the bone" of the negativistic Sensate world. As such, they are "at home" in that culture and appear to be valid to the Sensate mind. They easily infect Sensate individuals, including Sensate scientists and scholars. They are cultivated, approved, and glorified by the halo of "modern science." Their "facts" appear to be convincing; their logic persuasive; their "evidence" undeniable. Hence their success in the Sensate sociocultural world.

For the reason of non-congeniality, the positive "idealistic" theories are doomed to be the stepchildren in this Sensate culture of ours. They are destined to be "unpopular," and "unsuccessful" in the Sensate milieu; they appear to be "unconvincing," "unscientific," "prejudicial," and "superstitious" to Sensate society and to Sensate man.

When both kinds of these theories are carefully tested, their comparative validity becomes quite different from that determined by the extra-scientific, existential factor of their congeniality and non-congeniality with the dominant Sensate culture.

The purpose of the subsequent pages is to sum up a vast body of evidence in favor of the enormous power of creative love, friendship, and of non-violent and non-aggressive conduct in human affairs and social life. The corroborative facts are grouped in several classes, and a few typical cases are given in each class. The limited number is motivated by considerations of space: otherwise the cases of each class can be multiplied *ad libitum*.

2. LOVE AND KINDNESS STOP AGGRESSION AND ENMITY

"A friend of mine, an elderly Quaker lady, entered her Paris hotel room to find a burglar rifling her bureau drawers, where she had considerable jewelry and money. He had a gun which he brandished. She talked to him quietly, told him to go right ahead and help himself to anything she had, as obviously he needed it more than she did if he had to be stealing it. She even told him some places to look where there were valuables he had overlooked. Suddenly the man let out a low cry . . . and ran from the room taking nothing. The next day she received a letter from him in which he said, "I'm not afraid of hate. But you showed love and kindness. It disarmed me.'" (The fact communicated by C. Foster in her letter, November 7, 1951.)

"During the Revolutionary War William Rotch, a Friend, living on Nantucket Island, invited an enemy officer bent on plunder of the island to dinner. Thinking Rotch to be a loyalist, the officer asked him how and where to begin the plunder. Rotch replied: 'I don't know any better place for this to begin than here at my house, for I am better able to bear the loss than anyone else.' After meeting other persons in the village who had the same attitude as Rotch, the officer went back to his ship and left the island in its original condition." [3]

"Lotte Hoffman and her 16-year-old daughter were home in the suburbs of Berlin in 1945 when Russian soldiers burst into their room. She prayed silently, then walked over to her piano and began singing German folk-songs. Instead of shouting and threatening, the soldiers began to listen to the music. From

[3] A. Ruth Fry, *Victories without Violence* (published by the author, Suffolk, 1951), p. 19.

then on, as long as half-drunk troops were about, one or two Russian soldiers, armed, would sit up all night in Mrs. Hoffman's room to make sure that she and her daughter would be safe." [4]

In a detailed, twelve-page analysis of her own experience, a young American lady from California describes how on the eve of her departure from Colombo, in March, 1948, she was "cornered" in her hotel room by her neighbor in the adjacent room. The "neighbor" was determined to have sexual relations with her, willingly if she consented, to rape her if she opposed. In India the lady learned the method of "rational dealing with an opponent, omission of violence, necessity for understanding, 'love,' if the word is admissible in my situation." She applied this method. It required enormous courage and a steady nerve. With some difficulty it worked: she was able to convince the aggressor to go away without molesting her. "The struggle in my mind was too much for me. I was immensely fatigued," concludes the lady. (Personal communication to the author.)

The Brazilian government tried to destroy the Chavantes Indians (a tribe of 6,000 Indians in the northeast corner of Matto Grosso) in the eighteenth century. During the nineteenth century the government ignored them; missionaries failed also and several were killed. In 1907, General Candido Rondon founded the "Brazilian Indian Protection Service." Its policy was: "Pacification through Love." During his first attempt at contact General Rondon was badly injured, but ordered his men not to resist. In this behavioral way he established his policy: "Die if necessary, but never kill." He brought about the enactment of laws according to which no white Service man may kill an Indian even in self-defense; no Service man can carry arms in Indian territory. The "Protection Service"

[4] Allan A. Hunter, *Courage in Both Hands* (New York, 1951), p. 9; taken from William Hughes' journal, 1945, also reported by BBC, August 15, 1948, by W. Maude Brayshaw.

brought gifts to the Indians (by airplane and by leaving presents in temporarily abandoned villages).

Though a number of Service men were killed in the period of 1907-1946, no reprisals were made. The results of this policy have been more successful than any of the previous policies of extermination and aggression: several tribes of the Chavantes were pacified; others, formerly destructive, have become helpful to the government; still others can now be contacted without fatal results; Chavantes are now accepting gifts; the hostile actions of the white people are reduced. An expedition of twelve unarmed men in 1946 was succesful: an amicable meeting with 400 Indians took place. All in all, the policy of the "Pacification through Love" succeeded better than the aggressive policy.[5]

It is well known that in early America, in Pennsylvania, the Quakers, the Mennonites, the Moravians, the Schwenkfelders, all being adherents of non-violent resistance to evil, and all practicing the policy of unarmed friendship toward Indians, lived in peace with the Indians. Though a few, without offering resistance, were killed by the Indians, all in all, they suffered less from the Indians and lived in much greater peace with them than all the groups that fought and sought to destroy the Indians. The unarmed, peaceful policies of the Quakers and other pacifist groups were more successful in preventing and hindering the aggressive retaliation of the Indians than the militant, aggressive policies of other groups.[6]

When the Hun destroyer, Attila, in 452, was marching toward Rome, Pope Leo I went forth unarmed to meet the ruthless invader. Somehow he managed to gain an interview with Attila and make an appeal so powerful (and perhaps offered a

[5] Cf. H. B. White and W. Price, "Brazil Opens the West," *Saturday Evening Post*, March 15, 1947, pp. 24-25.
[6] Cf. W. J. Bender, *Nonresistance in Colonial Pennsylvania* (Scottdale, Mennonite Press, 1932).

considerable ransom, as some cynics conjecture) that Attila turned back, spared the city, and never returned. Whether or not Attila was well paid, the important fact is that an unarmed great spiritual leader could stop the terrible sacking of Rome.

In May 1922, in Russia, during the great famine, a band of plundering Kurds stopped a group of Quaker relief workers and started to take their food supplies. After discovering the nature of the help-rendering mission of the Quakers, the Kurds rode away without harming anyone or taking any of the supplies.[7]

At Pec, Serbia, during the famine, a young relief worker, assigned to drive oxcarts over robber-ridden mountain roads, refused a military escort. When robbers did stop him after many unmolested trips, he asked them to help him to transport the food to the starving people. Instead of attacking him, they helped him.[8]

In Berlin, in 1921, during the *putsch,* an Englishwoman, a Quaker leader, not only succeeded in making Communist and Government soldiers guard the Quaker supplies but, having introduced the enemy soldiers to one another in the storeroom, engaged them in pleasant conversation with one another and made them mutually friendly as they sat watching the supplies together.[9]

In New York City, in 1925, the treasurer of a Jewish hospital fund with $15,000 in his pocket was stopped by two robbers. When told that the money was for a hospital, the robbers threw in a ten-dollar bill of their own.

In 1924 in New York City a doctor of a slum district was stopped by two robbers. Informed that the doctor was attending

---

[7] Edward Thomas (ed.) *Quaker Adventures. Experiences of Twenty-Three Adventurers in International Understanding* (New York, London, 1921), p. 14.
[8] *Ibid.,* p. 15.
[9] *Ibid.,* pp. 15-16.

a sick woman in the area, they waited until his work was done and then escorted him to a safer part of the city.[10]

During and after the First World War nearly one thousand Quaker relief workers went unarmed into hostile countries. None met a violent death, nor were any of the relief goods plundered by robbers and the needy people.[11]

Hundreds of similar facts, up to the pacification of the civil war factions in Chinese villages and other places, are recorded in the annals of the Quaker relief missions in European countries, in Syria, in China, Nicaragua, Haiti, and other regions during and after the First World War up to the present time. Altruistic relief work of thousands of agents, acting often in the areas of bloody civil and international conflicts, has been able to overcome numerous aggressions, has calmed many enmities, and there have been very few, if any, violent deaths or serious harm among the workers.[12]

On December 31, 1937, in Shaktu Valley, Waziristan, British-led troops pulled out alive a few laborers of the Kakari clan who had been buried in a landslide. The clan hitherto fighting the British troops stopped its hostile actions and sniping; the act of saving a few laborers more successfully stopped the attacks of the Kakari than the military operations against them.[13]

During the extensive railroad building in the United States in the first half of the nineteenth century, engineer W. P. Thompson fired a trouble-making worker. This man threatened to kill Thompson. Thompson refused to go armed to retaliate against the worker. When Thompson surprised the worker was waiting in ambush for him, and later even gave him a very good reference as to his ability and character, the worker

[10] *Ibid.*, pp. 17-18.
[11] *Ibid.*, pp. 12-13.
[12] Cf. Many facts of this sort in *Quaker Adventures, passim.*
[13] A. Ruth Fry, *Victories Without Violence,* quoted, pp. 48-49.

became a changed man: he gave up his guns, stopped getting into arguments, and successfully advanced in his work for another railway.[14]

In the American Civil War the Shaker community of Pleasant Hill, Kentucky, was unharmed during the border violence inflicted at the time by John Morgan, a guerrilla leader: he had grown up to respect and admire the quiet, kindly Shakers.

Similar treatment was accorded to Jacob Gooff, Joseph Haughton, and other Quaker families during the rebellion in Ireland, about 1798; their reputation for kindness saved them and their property during the terrible persecutions and destruction around them.[15]

An American missionary, Merlin Bishop, politely but firmly refused to hand over the keys of an abandoned American university entrusted to his care in China to the Japanese officers demanding them. After several successful postponements the time finally came when an officer demanded the keys, threatening that the missionary would be shot. Bishop said he wished them no harm, but that he could not turn over the keys. Three men were selected and lined up with their rifles aimed at the missionary. He smiled and waited. "The officer seemed uncertain, the men uneasy. Then, one at a time they relaxed. Rifles lowered, sheepish grins replaced their looks of grim determination." But one of the soldiers apparently was disgusted at this outcome. He charged the missionary with a fixed bayonet on the end of his rifle. At the last instant the missionary dodged, grabbed the shorter soldier and the butt of the rifle, pulling him toward him. "Our glances locked and held for seconds that seemed ages long. Then I smiled down at him, and it was like a spring thaw melting the ice on a frozen river. The hatred vanished and, after a sheepish moment, he smiled back!" Then

[14] *Ibid.*, pp. 37-41.
[15] *Ibid.*, pp. 23-26.

Bishop gave them tea before they left on their return journey.[16]

A Japanese Christian, Osamu Ishiga, refusing conscription in Japan, was investigated and found to be neither a Communist nor a coward. "What baffled them [the authorities] was his sheer goodness, his vital personality. Finally they let him out of prison. There didn't seem to be any *other* way they could dispose of him!" (From a letter published in *Peace Notes* of the Fellowship of Reconciliation, April 14, 1949.)[17]

On May 8, 1945, in Dresden, Germany, Russians were entering the city, looting and sometimes raping. An American woman, a long-time resident of Dresden, calmly greeted the Russian soldier who stamped into her room, and shook hands with him. After examining the room he spied her watch. But instead of violently taking it, he cupped his hands and asked for it. She nodded "yes" as he emptied his pockets and rolled up his sleeves to show that he had picked up no loot. Then he left with a fleet kiss on her forehead and with a radiant smile.[18]

Incidents in the life of Bayard Rustin (present College Secretary, Fellowship of Reconciliation):

Once in a restaurant Rustin was ignored, after asking for a hamburger. Finally, attracting the attention of the woman proprietor, he succeeded in getting her to agree to his proposition: "He would sit before a cold hamburger, refusing to touch it for ten minutes. If any one came in and objected to the presence of a Negro in her restaurant, he would instantly leave without fuss." (p. 14). Before the time was up her resistance broke down and she brought him a hot dog and coffee. She then explained that her patrons did not want Negroes around because they were dirty. Instead of challenging this remark, Rustin said that it was true sometimes because many Negroes couldn't afford

---

[16] From *Fellowship,* January, 1945, Vol. II, No. 1, A. A. Hunter. Quoted in *Courage in Both Hands* (New York, 1951), pp. 5-7.
[17] Hunter, *op. cit.,* p. 7.
[18] *Ibid.,* p. 11.

baths in their houses. He gave other statements about the condition of the Negroes in the town, which the woman later took the trouble to verify. She then became interested in justice for the Negroes in the community and became a real friend to them.

While riding in an elevator in a Spokane hotel, Rustin was ordered by a white man to lace up his shoes. He did not object, performed the task, but then refused the offered tip, saying that he had done it not for money but because he had assumed the man needed help. The white man was apologetic and invited Bayard to his room to talk about racial problems.[19]

Three Dutch sisters were in danger since they were sheltering a Jew, for the Gestapo men were quartered across the street from them. Nevertheless, when a Gestapo man called on them, they invited him in since they decided that Jesus would have done so. The Gestapo man then made it a practice to take part in their evening prayers and songs. At first the German had hated the Jews. As time went on the arguments and behavior of the sisters began to tell. At his last visit the German grew white when the younger sister said that the "Jews are to the Lord as the apple of the eye." He whipped out his revolver, but instead of using it, he handed it over saying he was a sinner. After their evening prayer and hymn he left. They never saw him again.[20]

When the Kingsley Hall neighborhood house was threatened by attack from persons drawn from nearby saloons by a disgruntled lady who blamed the Hall for her trouble with her daughter, the leader, Miss Muriel Lester, let them come in, heard the tirade of "Mrs. Smith," then asked all to join in prayer about it. The drunks took off their hats during the prayer. Miss Lester offered her arm to the surprised lady immediately after the prayer, and marched out of the house, fol-

[19] *Ibid.*, pp. 13-17.
[20] *Ibid.*, pp. 21-23.

lowed by all the rest. No damage was done, and Mrs. Smith sobered up on the way home. She declared her eternal friendship for Miss Lester, from which she has never wavered.[21]

During the Nazi regime Wilhelm Mensching, pastor in Petzen, Germany, was openly against the Nazis. He refused to say "Heil Hitler" or to put the Nazi flag in his church. When he was told that a certain Nazi was going to have him thrown out of the church, he went straight to the man and told him that his allegiance was to Christ, that since the Nazi now had the relevant information, he could get the pastor kicked out. But the Nazi refused to take action. Though Mensching openly prayed for the enemies, kept in touch with English friends, voted against the Nazis, etc., he was never arrested. The mayor and all the people loved him and told the Nazis that he would not betray anyone but be friends to all.[22]

When awakened one night by a professional robber, a Canadian named Michael was unafraid, began to talk with the robber, and gave him some coffee and a sandwich. The robber shook hands with him when he left, and instead of taking something, left his gun with Michael.

In a mopping-up operation during the First World War, he once came face to face with a German fighter. Michael immediately walked toward the enemy, his rifle on his shoulder, smiling and exclaiming "Kamerad!" The puzzled German advanced toward him with his bayonet, but stopped just a few feet away as Michael continued to smile and tried to speak German. Michael said, "Liebe mannen, alles mannen." The incredulous German asked, "Alles mannen? Deutsch?" "Ja, alles mannen," answered Michael. Gradually the German came to understand his position and broke out with "Freund! Freund!" They chatted for a while; then each went his own way.[23]

[21] *Ibid.*, pp. 28-29.
[22] *Ibid.*, pp. 29-30.
[23] *Ibid.*, pp. 33-37.

Joyohiko Kagawa in Japan had just finished speaking at a church service. Ten hooligans arose and attacked him with large bamboo sticks. He stood with no change of expression on his face as the blows fell and the blood streamed. When they stopped, Kagawa led the congregation in the closing prayer. He then invited the hooligans into his study to talk to them. Before long they were apologizing.

Kagawa "has so much security inside that he can afford to go without any outside." Alone in his tiny room in the Shinkawa slums, he was awakened one night by a drunk or half-drunk gangster, with sword uplifted. Kagawa got to his knees and bowed his head in prayer as he awaited the blow. Instead, the man said, "Kagawa, do you love me?" Kagawa answered, "Yes, I do." Soon the man said, "Here's a present," and he left Kagawa his sword.

Hearing of the march of 10,000 destruction-bent strikers toward armed police and soldier-guarded dockyards, Kagawa abruptly closed his sermon, and averted the impending slaughter by checking and directing the first row of marchers down a side street. Single-handed he faced the strikers and as the first row approached him, he looked into the eyes of each, praying "Let there be peace." They swerved down a side street and the dockyards were left untouched. No shots were fired; the union was saved.[24]

During the *satyagraha* campaign in Vykom, Travancore Province, South India, Brahmins refused to let Untouchables walk along a highway near their quarters. An Untouchable and a young Christian started it off by walking down the road. Both were beaten. They did it again and were arrested. Others took their places until authorities stopped the arrests and put a line of police across the road. Then the *satyagrahis* started to stand opposite the policemen in an attitude of prayer. They went on six-hour shifts and persisted in their non-violence despite

[24] *Ibid.*, pp. 40-43.

threats, insults, etc. A year and four months later the Brahmins gave in and opened up not only this road but other roads in the province to the Untouchables.[25]

During World War II a young American was being marched at bayonet point toward Japanese lines. He began to speak Bible passages and sing hymns as he went along to build up his courage. As he found strength in his voice and soul, his singing became contagiously relaxed. Soon his Japanese captor was walking beside him and singing along with him. When the hymn ended they stopped and swapped experiences. They prayed together. Then instead of killing his prisoner, the Japanese decided not to kill any more. The two made their way together toward the American camp.[26]

Kees Boecke, Dutch Quaker, teacher, missionary, and war resister, had allowed a Jew to sleep in his office during the Nazi occupation. It turned out that this man was active in the underground, had been caught, and now the Gestapo was waiting for Boecke in his office. He admitted allowing the Jew to sleep there, saying that he followed a different faith from theirs. He said he believed in the brotherhood of men and taught this in his school. Despite the finding of an article he had written for post-war publication which condemned dictatorship and the Nazi occupation, no harm came to him.[27]

A German orphanage outside of Berlin was wanted for quarters by the Russians. But the director of the school, Isa Gruner, had planned how to maintain the school should this happen. When the Russians came they were greeted by the youngsters, who had learned Russian songs. Soon the soldiers were singing

[25] Cf. similar facts in Allan A. Hunter, *Three Trumpets Sound;* C. F. Andrews, "Mahatma Gandhi," *The Canadian Student,* Vol. 12, No. 1; Richard Gregg, *The Power of Non-violence* (Lippincott, 1934); J. C. Winslow and Verrier Elwyn, *Gandhi, the Dawn of Indian Freedom* (Revell, 1931).
[26] *Fellowship,* November, 1945.
[27] Hunter, *op. cit.,* pp. 48-50.

with them. When the officer said the buildings would have to be cleared out, Isa said that the schoolteachers would take care of the Russians—cook, wash, iron, etc. She had a sign put up saying that the school was under the protection of the Russian soldiers. This plan worked for nine months. Then another group of Russian soldiers came who wanted all of the buildings for the soldiers. Their officer refused to listen when Isa said the school was under the protection of the Russian army. Then she began to cry. The other teachers cried, as did the children. The officer couldn't stand this and told them to go back to their cottages. Then he and his soldiers left.[28]

Mr. Arima was administrator of the Kosuge prison of Tokyo. Before a man was released Arima would often find a job for him. He treated and fed the men well, gave them interesting things to do, both in skills and in recreation. When a released man broke faith and was returned to prison, he was treated to new clothes and a good meal, and once more became a cooperative member of the group. The results of this kind of administration were tested in the great earthquake of 1923. Walls of the prison were broken. Arima went around letting the prisoners out of the crumbling cells. Although there was nothing to hold them any more, the prisoners rallied around their warden and remained true to his trust in them. The detachment of soldiers that arrived to guard them was refused by Arima. To prove his faith, the roll was called and practically every one of the 1300 was there to answer the test.[29]

Leonard, a 4-year-old member of a nursery school group, has been very irritable and out of sorts recently. Aggressive behavior is unusual in this particular group, and the children have not responded in kind to his attacks against them. They have discussed and lamented his "trouble" and agreed that he needs to be treated "extra nice." One afternoon when it was time to

---

[28] *Ibid.*, pp. 56-58.
[29] Allan A. Hunter, *Out of the Far East*, Friendship Press, 1934.

THE POWER OF CREATIVE LOVE

go home, he refused to put on his snow-suit. When the teacher ignored his angry demands for her help, he began to flail the children near him with the pants of his suit. The teacher removed him to the corridor. There he cried, stomped, and hit at everyone who passed. The teacher accidentally stepped on his scarf as she passed him. At this he dissolved in tears, and Eileen, who had just been struck hard on the shin by the buckle on one of his pants straps, rushed to his rescue. Firmly but soothingly she said, "Sit down, Leonard, I'm going to help you." And as she did so, three other children came to help, too. Together they pushed and poked the placated child into his wraps, while he repeatedly sighed, "These are my friends." [30]

More than 23 centuries ago, Moh-Tze walked for ten days and ten nights, according to the story, to reach the office of a state engineer who had invented a new weapon and was making plans to invade a neighboring state. Moh-Tze convinced the inventor to give up the plan to start a war.[31]

Telemachus, a monk in Asia Minor, made his way to Rome, a thousand miles away, to see what he could do to stop the slaughter of human life in the huge Roman gladiatorial shows. In the middle of a fight he ran from his seat in the amphitheatre and called upon the combatants to cease their attempts to kill each other. The furious spectators rushed in and beat him to death with sticks and stones. But the sacrifice had its effect on Honorius, the Emperor. He issued a rescript forbidding all gladiatorial combats. The evil spectacle was never held again.[32]

Thomas Lurting, a former war hero of the British Navy, had become a Quaker and was on his civilian ship when it was captured by Turkish pirates. His captain and some others were

---

[30] Observation made in Hecht House Nursery School, February, 1952.
[31] Hu Shih, *The Development of Logical Method in China*, Oriental Book Co., Shanghai, 1922.
[32] Sir Ernest Bennett, *Christian Pacifist*, April, 1942, pp. 68-69.

taken to the Turkish ship, leaving Lurting and the crew behind with only ten Turks to guard them. By a skillful maneuver Lurting managed to get the Turks locked into the hold. Then he sailed into port, planning to release the Turks there. Upon regaining his command, the captain decided to deceive Lurting and sell the captured Turks as slaves. But Lurting heard of this plan and, with three helpers, loaded the Turks into a small boat and rowed them to shore, where they were set free. There they parted "in great love." After that Quakers alone were allowed by the people of that region to come among them without hostility.[33]

Mrs. Grace Olive Wiley feels perfectly safe handling deadly rattlers and cobras. She attributes her years of success in handling these snakes to an application of the Golden Rule. She tries to "communicate confidence" to them until a relationship of mutual trust is built up.

When wolves were needed for the Hollywood movie "The Call of the Wild," Larry Trimble undertook to train 20 of them. They were let loose in a twenty-acre stockade. Larry would leave pieces of meat out in the open, then curl up in his sleeping bag in the same area, defenseless but confident. Before long the wolves were eating out of his hand and sleeping within a few yards of him.[34]

Helen Keller insisted against being given warnings upon becoming more familiar with a lion, which she had heard of but could not see or hear. She walked into a lion's cage without fear and inquiringly knelt before the surprised lion, who strangely offered no resistance to her touch. As she explored the lion's muscles, mane, paws, tail, etc., it roared (but Helen didn't hear); nevertheless, he made no effort to stop her as if he sensed the friendliness of his visitor.[35]

[33] M. A. Best, *Rebel Saints,* New York, 1925.
[34] A. Hunter, *op. cit.,* pp. 69-70.
[35] Margaret T. Applegarth, *Right Here, Right Now* (New York, 1950), pp. 11-12.

Sundar Singh had become a wandering Christian *sadhu*, living a dedicated life of voluntary poverty in India. A leopard was on the loose near a village where Sundar happened to be. The villagers were frantically searching it out, but Sundar sat defenseless and alone in a clearing near his host's house. As the night wore on, his host became anxious for him, and looked out the window just in time to see the leopard crawling toward Sundar. Too late to call out he stared in wonder as Sundar reached out and serenely stroked the leopard's head. When he came into the house and answered his host's questions, Sundar said, "Why should the leopard harm me? I am not his enemy."

When a listener once struck Sundar Singh a savage blow, Sundar merely washed off the wound with water from a ditch and came back singing to his audience. By the end of the hour the man who had struck him wanted to go along with Sundar.

In the bandit-ridden mountains Sundar was once attacked, but upon seeing the tranquillity on his face, the bandits changed their minds and invited him to their cave for a chat. Before he left, the leader had become a Christian.[36]

The Maori in New Zealand had no weapons to fight the white imperialists taking possession of their land. One wise leader, upon hearing that the English were marching to attack his village, summoned his people together and told them to prepare for a feast, to meet and welcome the soldiers with songs, dances, and games. The soldiers were baffled by their reception and followed the procession into the village, where they were met by the chief with friendliness and hospitality. They could do nothing but accept the spirit of their hosts. They finally withdrew, leaving the tribe in possession of the land, and never made another expedition against them.[37]

Baiko San had been asked to become priest for her village

[36] C. F. Andrews, *Sadhu Sundar Singh* (New York, 1934).
[37] *The Messenger of Peace,* supplement to the *American Friend,* April 16, 1931.

in China after the previous priest—her husband—had died. One night she was awakened in her little shrine by a robber demanding the money from the last night's meeting. She calmly said she would not give it to him. When he threatened her with a sword, she said she was old and ready to die, but that she was concerned about him and his future should he kill her. Then she said that he could have her own personal money given her by the villagers, told him where it was, and went back to sleep. The next morning she found that none of the money had been touched.[38]

When Richard Baxter was working in an English mine, he decided to turn over a new leaf, not to get drunk and not to get into fights any more. On his job one day he found a fellow worker bullying one of the small boys in charge of a coal-carrying wagon. After Richard had helped the boy get back the wagon, the worker growled that he felt like smacking Richard in the face. Richard told him to go ahead, and the man hit him several times without receiving any resistance. When he saw this worker the next time he went down into the mine, the worker broke out into tears and asked for forgiveness. Richard said he had forgiven him. They shook hands and became friends.[39]

During the Civil War William Hockett was drafted into a North Carolina regiment. He refused to participate in the military system and was finally ordered to be shot. As the rifles were raised he raised his arms and said, "Father, forgive them; for they know not what they do." Not a trigger was pulled; the guns were lowered without orders. Members of the company were heard to say they could not kill such a man.[40]

In the year 1917, in Russia, bands of ruffians roved Southern

---

[38] Michi Kawai, *My Lantern* (Tokyo, 1930), pp. 6-11.
[39] William James, *The Varieties of Religious Experience*, New York, 1903, pp. 281-83.
[40] Allan A. Hunter, *Youth's Adventure*, New York, 1925.

Russia, marauding, raping, killing. A Mennonite community, though long pacifist, was frightened into arming to protect its women and children and "to fight fire with fire." The attack came; many were killed, the women raped and brutally treated. After the invaders left, a council was held and it was decided to go back to the old way. The next time the raiders came the men went out to meet them without guns. Instead, they knelt and prayed for their loved ones and also for their enemies. "The impact of this spirit got through. It reached the conscience of their attackers. The marauders apparently sensed that they were up against a superior even if invisible power. They left and did not return." [41]

When Dr. Theodore Pennell went into the Northwest Frontier in India, a price was put on his head by the local Mowlahs (Mohammedan clergy). As soon as Pennell found out the name of one of these persons, he paid the man a visit. The surprised Mowlah could not carry out his own orders—after all, you can't stick a knife into a guest—you must be hospitable. So Pennell became the Pathans' friend and lived unarmed among them for years. The Commander of the British army on the frontier said his presence was worth two battalions for the peace which followed his presence.[42]

An old Hindu and his servants stopped to rest in a spot infested by robbers. Despite his servants' warnings the old man sat down alone to watch the setting sun. A robber, believing the old man to be wealthy, crept up on him with a dagger in his hand. The old man's eyes turned on the robber with quietness and love. The surprised robber dropped the dagger and fell at the man's feet, confessing his sin. Instead of admonishing the

---

[41] A. Hunter, *op. cit.*, p. 77.
[42] J. H. Franklin, *Ministers of Mercy*, Chap. I (Missionary Education Movement, New York, 1919); A. M. Pennell, *Pennell of the Afghan Frontier* (New York, 1920), p. 6.

robber, the old man rose and threw his arms around him indicating that the robber was now his disciple. The robber became a new man and lived a life of service.[43]

A converted New Hebrides chieftain, an ex-cannibal, sent a message to a fellow-chieftain that he and four attendants would pay a visit the next Sunday to tell of their new ideas. He received the answer that if anyone came trying to preach to them at any time, all would be killed. The chieftain sent another message saying that he had learned to return good for evil, and would appear unarmed with his attendants the next Sunday. Again the blunt reply was that if they came they would be killed. When the chieftain and his little band appeared, walking toward his village, the non-cooperative chief begged them to leave, but nothing would stop the chief with his message. Soon spears began to fall around them; before long they were dodging and expertly catching the close ones. Out of wonder the villagers stopped throwing their spears and listened to the Christian chief. Eventually the chieftain with his people became pupils of this new way of living.[44]

In the 1905 Russian Revolution in Southern Russia, a small Mennonite community was threatened by the rebels, who were destroying everything in their path. One family met the situation by preparing a good rich supper the day of the expected raid. The husband asked his wife to set the table for guests, and sent the children to bed. When the band appeared and asked the father to surrender, he invited them in to the prepared dinner, saying that anything of his was theirs, but that they must want refreshment first. They hesitated, then sat down to eat. After the supper the father showed them beds he had prepared in the next room. After their sleep the leader ap-

[43] C. F. Andrews, *What I Owe to Christ* (New York, 1932), pp. 245-6.
[44] William James, *The Varieties of Religious Experience*, (New York, 1903), p. 359.

peared again, this time smiling, and said: "We have to go. We came to kill you, but we can't."[45]

In an experimental study of the Harvard Research Center in Creative Altruism, we set a task to change the inimical relationship between members of each pair of Harvard and Radcliffe students into an amicable one. Five pairs of mutually hating students were dealt with. The method of good deeds was selected for the aimed transformation. One of the students of each pair was persuaded to start to do some kind deed to the disliked partner. Within a period of some four months the inimical relationships in all five pairs were replaced by amicable ones. Performance of small deeds of kindness (inviting to dances, giving tickets for the theater, helping in the study work, teaching the other party to crochet, etc.) began to change the performer and then the other party in replacing their dislike by better understanding and then friendship.[46]

In another experimental study of changing an attitude of dislike of certain nurses by certain patients of the Boston Psychopathic Hospital, the technique of good deeds and unfailing kindness by the disliked nurses toward the disliking patients succeeded fully in replacing the previous antagonisms by friendly relationships.[47]

Conclusion: The foregoing facts and incidents have intentionally been selected with a view to being diverse in their concrete forms. In spite of their diversity, they all show the power of love subduing the force of enmity, ag-

[45] A. Hunter, *op. cit.*, pp. 82-83.
[46] Cf. J. Mark Thompson, "Experimentation with the Technique of Good Deeds in Transformation of Inimical into Amicable Relationships," to be published in P. Sorokin (ed.), *Symposium on Techniques of Altruistic and Spiritual Transformation* (Beacon Press, Boston, 1953).
[47] Cf. R. W. Hyde and H. Kandler, "Altruism in Psychiatric Nursing," to be published in the same *Symposium*.

gression, or hate. Facts of that sort can be multiplied *ad libitum*. In the experience of everyone of us similar events have probably happened many times. Sometimes they become unforgettable; at other times they are forgotten. Whether remembered or forgotten, they occur. When they are registered at least as carefully as the facts of enmity overcoming friendship, the occasions on which love overpowers animosity appear to be much more frequent than we habitually think. Facts of this sort give a firm basis for the contention that unselfish love, true kindness, and friendship have real power, and that this power is much greater than Sensate individuals believe. Subsequent series of empirical data tremendously reinforce this conclusion.

3. LOVE BEGETS LOVE, HATE BEGETS HATE

Evidence of the power of love is next supplied by innumerable facts showing that unselfish love is at least as "contagious" as hate, and influences human behavior as tangibly as hate does. If and when an individual or group approaches other persons or groups in a friendly manner, the respondents' answer to such an approach is also kindly in an overwhelming majority of cases. And the frequency of the friendly response to the friendly approach is at least as high as that of an inimical response to an aggressive approach.

Of numerous observations of this uniformity, only a few typical cases can be mentioned here. R. W. Hyde and H. Eichorn studied the approaches and responses of a group of patients of the Boston Psychopathic Hospital, and obtained the following results: to friendly approaches the respondents reacted in a friendly manner in 73 percent of actions-reactions; in 16 percent they responded in an aggressive manner; and in 11 percent in a neutral way. To aggressive approaches the respondents answered aggressively in 69 percent, in a friendly manner in 25 percent, and indifferently in 6 percent. The authors remark that the 16 percent aggressive response to the friendly approaches is possibly due to the "superficiality of friendly approach hiding an undercurrent of hostility or of disinterestedness." Likewise, a friendly response to the seemingly aggressive approach "may have been accepted by the recipients as compliments regarding their sexual potency." Whatever the cause of the aggressive response to the friendly approach and of the friendly response to the aggressive approach, the main rule that love begets love and begets it as frequently as hate generates hate is clear from the data. The percentage of the friendly response to the friendly approach is even slightly higher than that of the unfriendly response to the unfriendly approach.[48]

In Sorokin's study of the relationship between each of 548 Harvard and Radcliffe students and his or her "best friend," the friendship was initiated in 23.7 percent of cases by an act of kindness, help, sympathy, and care of one or of both parties; in the remaining 76.3 percent of the cases it was due to the desirable traits, and mutual supplementation of the values and experiences of the parties involved. There was not a single case of a friendship initiated by aggression of one or of both parties. The inimical relationship between each of these students and his or her "worst enemy" was started in 48.1 percent

[48] Cf. H. Eichorn and R. W. Hyde, "Interaction in the Mental Hospital," in P. Sorokin (ed.), *Explorations in Altruistic Love and Behavior* (Boston, 1950), pp. 258-260.

of the cases by an action of aggression or unfriendliness of one or of both parties involved. In the remaining 51.9 percent of the cases the enmity was due to the undesirable personal traits, to the incompatibility of the values, ideals, and aspirations of the parties involved. Here again friendliness tends to beget friendliness and aggression generates enmity.[49]

In another, more detailed investigation of how friendship started and developed with "the best friend" of each of 73 Harvard and Radcliffe students, and how the enmity with "the worst enemy" of each of these students grew, the results were fairly similar to the above: 24.2 percent of friendships were started by actions of kindness, generosity, help, or sympathy of one or of both parties; 42.7 percent of enmities were started by aggressive and inimical actions of one or of both parties. The friendship of the remaining percentage was due to hidden and somewhat milder actions of sympathy and mutual supplementation of the parties involved, while the enmity in the remaining percentage was due to a lack of sympathy, indifference, and a milder form of animosity of the parties in question.[50]

Here again the emergence and development of either friendship or animosity follow the formula: love begets love, enmity produces enmity.

In a number of other clinical, observational, and experimental studies similar results were obtained.

A group of 10-year-old children under autocratic and

[49] P. Sorokin, "Affiliative and Hostile Tendencies of College Students," *Explorations,* quoted, pp. 289-90.
[50] P. Sorokin, "Dynamics of Interpersonal Friendship and Enmity," to be published in P. Sorokin (ed.), *Symposium on the Techniques of Altruistic and Spiritual Transformation.*

aggressive conditions displayed thirty times more frequent hostility and eight times more frequent aggression among its members than the same group under non-aggressive and democratic conditions.[51]

M. E. Bonney's study has shown that the technique of praising, complimenting, helping, and initiating friendly discussion is the best procedure in "how to make friends."[52]

In M. D. Fite's experiment the technique of helping aggressive children to find a good solution to their immediate problems proved to be more successful in curing their aggressiveness than the techniques of reproof, repression, and punishment.[53]

In a large number of other investigations the rule of love begetting love has been well confirmed.[54]

Most of the material given above and further on well supports the basic rule: friendship generates friendship and animosity creates enmity. The rule means that any genuine (and adequate) [55] love or friendship effectively (though not in every case) changes the human mind and overt behavior in a friendly direction toward the friendly acting person(s). In this inner and overt trans-

[51] Cf. K. Lewin, R. Lippitt, R. K. White, "Patterns of Aggressive Behavior," *Journal of Social Psychology*, 10: 271-299, 1939.
[52] M. E. Bonney, "A Sociometric Study," *Sociometry*, 9:21-47, 1946.
[53] M. D. Fite, "Aggressive Behavior in Young Children," *Genetic Psychology Monographs*, 22:151-319, 1940.
[54] Cf. L. Bender, S. Keiser, and P. Schilder, "Studies in Aggressiveness," II, *Genetic Psychology Monographs*, 18:546-564, 1938; G. H. Reeve, "General Principles," *American Journal of Orthopsychiatry*, 13:411-414, 1943.
[55] Cf. on the meaning of "adequate" love, P. Sorokin, "Love: Its Aspects," etc., in P. Sorokin, *Explorations*, quoted, pp. 27-30.

formation the power of love seems to be as effective as the power of hate or animosity.

4. LOVE AS AN IMPORTANT FACTOR OF VITALITY AND LONGEVITY

Other conditions being equal, and of two persons with identical biological organisms, the kind and friendly person tends to live longer and to have better health than the unkind, and especially the hate-possessed individual. Love in its various forms proves to be one of the most important factors of longevity and good health.

The first important evidence for this is supplied by the duration of life of the Christian Saints. An overwhelming majority of these Saints were eminent altruists. Sorokin's study of 3,090 Christian and Catholic Saints and 415 Russian Orthodox Saints from the beginning of Christianity up to the present time has shown that they had notably longer life-duration than their unsaintly and less altruistic contemporaries. Though the duration of life of 37 percent of these Saints was cut off by premature death through martyrdom; though most of them lived ascetic lives, denying satisfaction of many bodily needs; though many of them lived in non-hygienic conditions; and though the average life-duration of the populations in the centuries before the nineteenth was notably lower than that of the United States population in 1920—despite all these adverse conditions, the life-duration of the Saints as a group was somewhat higher than that of the American population in 1920.[56]

[56] P. Sorokin, *Altruistic Love* (Boston, 1950), pp. 100-101.

On the other hand, the life-giving and life-sustaining power of love is strikingly demonstrated by the fact of *suicide*. We know now that the main cause of suicide is psychosocial isolation of the individual, his state of being lonely in the human universe, of not loving or caring for anybody and not being loved by anybody. Each time the love-ties of a person break down, especially when they break down abruptly; when his attachments to other persons weaken; when he becomes an unattached and disattached human atom in the universe, his chances of suicide increase. Each time one's love and attachment to fellow-men multiply and grow stronger, one's chances for suicide decrease.[57] This means that love is indeed the intensest vital force, the central core of life itself. Further on, this conclusion will be reinforced by other basic evidence.

5. CURATIVE POWER OF LOVE

This conclusion is well corroborated by a vast body of evidence that demonstrates a tangible curative power of love in regard to certain physical and mental disorders. Modern psychosomatic medicine correctly views the strong emotional disturbances, especially of an aggressive, inimical, hateful, and antagonistic kind, as one of the basic factors of cardiovascular, respiratory, gastro-intestinal, eliminative, skin, endocrine, genito-urinary, and other disturbances. These are also basically involved in such ailments as epilepsy and headache. "The great anatomist, John Hunter, is reputed to have said concerning his angina pectoris, 'My life is at the mercy of any rascal who can make

---

[57] Cf. on the factors of suicide, P. Sorokin, *Society, Culture, and Personality* (New York, 1947), p. 8 ff. See there also the literature on this problem.

me angry.' "[58] Among other things, a strong hateful, angry, inimical emotion robs one of his peace of mind and through that (and other ways) undermines one's health and vitality. On the other hand, emotions of love, sympathy, and friendship tend to build one's peace of mind, one's equanimity toward one's fellow men and the world at large; for this and other reasons they exert revitalizing and curative effects upon the organism and its disturbances.

For babies motherly love is a vital necessity. Deprived of warm love, they sicken and die as quickly as they sicken and die because of infection or hunger or improper diet. One of the latest studies along this line is that of René A. Spitz, who observed and filmed the death of 34 foundlings in a foundling home. These infants had all their needs cared for except that of motherly love. Its lack was sufficient to make them sicken and die. The whole process of the withering of their vitality was filmed by Dr. Spitz. After three months of separation from their parents, the babies lost sleep and became shrunken, whimpering and trembling. After an additional two months, most of them began to look like idiots. Twenty-seven foundlings died in their first year of life; seven in the second. Twenty-one other children lived longer but "were so altered that thereafter they could be classified only as 'idiots.' "[59]

---

[58] Cf. on psychosomatic disturbances, L. J. Saul, "Physiological Effects of Emotional Tensions," in J. McV. Hunt (ed.), *Personality and the Behavior Disorders* (New York, 1944), pp. 269-305; see there for other literature.

[59] *New York Times*, April 27, 1952. Cf. similar cases in Ashley Montagu's book, *On Being Human* (New York, 1950).

The therapeutic power of love is especially important in preventing and healing mental and moral disturbances. As we shall see in the subsequent sections of this paper, the grace of love in the form of both loving and being loved is the most important condition for newly born babies to grow into morally and mentally sound human beings. Deprivation of love in childhood ordinarily leads such unfortunate persons to moral and mental disturbances in their youth and adult periods.

In our age of "psychoneuroses" and of considerable juvenile delinquency, the Mennonite and the Hutterite communities in the United States show either no or the lowest quota of delinquents, criminals, and mentally sick persons. The chief reason for this is that these communities try to practice in the interrelationship of their members the precepts of the Sermon on the Mount; they not only preach love but realize it in their daily behavior. No member of the communities is deprived of love, and all are united into one real brotherhood.[60]

The power of love, sympathy, empathy, and understanding appears to be the main curative agent in diverse therapies of mental disorders. It is exceedingly difficult to establish just how curative the various psychiatric techniques are. The difficulties are due to a lack of objective criteria of improvement, diagnosis, record-keeping, etc. Various attempts to measure the curative effects of diverse psychiatric therapies give discrepant results, from a very

---

[60] Cf. the facts and evidence in J. W. Eaton, R. J. Weil, and Bert Kaplan, "The Hutterite Mental Health Study," *Mennonite Quarterly Review,* January, 1951; B. W. Clark, "The Hutterian Communities," *Journal of Political Economy,* 32: 357-374, 468-486, 1924; L. E. Deets, *The Hutterites: A Study of Social Cohesion* (Gettysburg, 1939).

low percentage of the patients showing temporary and slight improvement up to some 40 to 60 percent of the cases in psychoneurotic, sexual, and character disorders; and much lower in epilepsy, migraine, stammering, chronic alcoholism, and psychoses.[61]

Regardless of the uncertainty and contradictoriness of the curative results of various psychiatric methods, on one vital point the psychiatrists seem to be in essential agreement, namely, *that the main curative agent in all the diverse psychiatric techniques is the "acceptance" of the patient by the therapist, the rapport of empathy, sympathy, kindness, and love established between the therapist and the patient.* In other words, the essence of the curative therapy consists in the patient's "exposure" to the "radiation" of understanding, kindness, and love of the therapist, instead of the "atmosphere" of "rejection," "enmity," "reproofs," and punishment in which the patient usually lives.

Concluding his study of the percentages and the degress of improvement of patients subjected to various psychiatric therapies, K. E. Appel concludes that "the therapeutic statistics of psychiatry appear to justify . . . that any therapy [in the sense of friendly rapport between the therapist

---

[61] Cf. the results in R. P. Knight, "Evaluation of the Results of Psychoanalytic Therapy," *American Journal of Psychiatry*, 98:434-446, 1941; K. E. Appel, "Psychiatric Therapy," in J. McV. Hunt (ed.), *Personality and the Behavior Disorders* (New York, 1944), pp. 1107-1163; L. Kessel and Harold T. Hyman, "The Value of Psychoanalysis as a Therapeutic Procedure," *Journal of American Medical Assn.*, 101: 1612-1615 (1933); A. Salter, *The Case Against Psychoanalysis* (New York, 1952); C. R. Rogers, N. J. Raskin, and others, "A Coordinated Research in Psychotherapy," *Journal of Consulting Psychology*, 13: 149-220, 1949.

and the patient] *is* in itself more fundamental than the type employed. There is something basically effective in the process of therapy in general which is independent of the methods employed." [62]

The same conclusion is reached by F. E. Fiedler[63] in his studies of the effectiveness of various psychiatric methods and especially of the "ideal therapeutic relationship." These studies show that in spite of wide differences in the theories and specific techniques of various psychiatric methods, the curative results of expert psychiatrists are fairly similar and the eminent psychiatrists of different schools all agree in what is the best or "the ideal therapeutic relationship." It is marked by the following characteristics, which speak for themselves. Complete empathy between the therapist and the patient. Good rapport. Therapist sticks closely to the patient's problems. The patient feels free to say what he likes. An atmosphere of mutual trust and confidence. The therapist accepts all feelings which the patient expresses as completely normal and understandable (according to the old precept: "To understand all is to forgive all"). The patient assumes an active role in his own improvement. A full understanding and sympathy between the parties.

In contrast to this "ideal therapeutic relationship," the worst and least effective therapy is marked by a punitive therapist, making the patient feel rejected, having little respect for the patient; by impersonal, cold, often inimical relationship of the parties; by treatment of the patient

---

[62] K. E. Appel, "Psychiatric Therapy," quoted, p. 1155.
[63] F. E. Fiedler, "The Concept of an Ideal Therapeutic Relationship," quoted, pp. 239-245.

as a child or as an irresponsible, dangerous, stupid, and inferior person.[64]

In another study of the problem Fiedler concludes:

"This investigation supports the theory that the relationship [of understanding, communication, and sympathy between the therapist and the patient] *is* therapy, that the goodness of therapy is a function of the goodness of the therapeutic relationship [in the sense of 'the ideal therapeutic relationship'] . . . that the patients who cannot establish interpersonal relationships with others do not seem to improve as a result of psychotherapy."

A patient must have "support, security, and understanding," as well as "acceptance and warmth" from the therapist if any cure can occur, concludes S. G. Estes in his study of this problem.[65]

"The positive transference," that is, the affectionate and warm feeling of the patient toward the therapist in contradistinction to "the negative transference with its feeling of hostility" is generally regarded as the necessary condition for improvement of the patient. "When the transference is positive, the analytic work proceeds smoothly. . . . Sometimes a negative transference dominates. . . . Then the work goes on slowly, with difficulty, without signs of benefit to the patient." [66]

One of the patients sums up the situation as follows:

[64] F. E. Fiedler, "A Comparison of Therapeutic Relationships in Psychoanalytic, Nondirective, and Adlerian Therapy," *Journal of Consulting Psychology*, 14: 436-445, 1950.
[65] S. G. Estes, "The Therapeutic Relationship in the Dynamics of Cure," *Journal of Consulting Psychology*, 12:76-81, 1948.
[66] R. W. White, *The Abnormal Personality* (New York, 1948), p. 334.

"As a result of my own experience as a client, I am convinced that the counselor's complete acceptance, his expression of the attitude of wanting to help the client, and his warmth of spirit expressed by his wholehearted giving of himself to the client in complete cooperation with everything the client does or says are basic in this ['the client-centered'] type of therapy." [67]

C. R. Rogers describes the process of curing as follows:

"The client moves from the experiencing of himself as an unworthy, unacceptable, and unlovable person to the realization that he is accepted, respected, and loved, in this limited relationship with the therapist. 'Loved' has here perhaps its deepest and most general meaning—that of being deeply understood and deeply accepted." [68]

Similar is the conclusion of the competent therapists of practically all the schools of psychiatry.[69]

---

[67] C. R. Rogers, *Client-Centered Therapy* (Boston, 1951), pp. 37-38.
[68] *Ibid.*, p. 159. Cf. also pp. 51-52, 69, 74, 158-161, and *passim*. Like many other therapists Rogers correctly indicates the ineffectiveness of a faked, insincere, sham-love or friendship. Such a simulacrum of love does not work.
[69] Cf. K. Menninger, *Love Against Hate* (New York, 1942), pp. 6, 128-29, 136, 262, and *passim*. Where Menninger repeats the Freudian concept of love, he unduly reduces it to the sexual variety. Fortunately, in many places of his book Menninger forgets Freudian concepts and gives an analysis of love and of its functions far more adequate than Freudian misconceptions.

Cf. also the studies of J. Seeman, E. T. Sheerer, D. Stock, G. Haigh, A. E. Hoffman, A. C. Carr, in "A Coordinated Research in Psychotherapy," quoted; P. E. Kauffman and V. C. Raimy, "Two Methods of Assessing Therapeutic Process," *Journal of Abnormal and Social Psychology*, 44:379-385, 1949; E. G. Boring, "Was This Analysis a Success," *Journal of Abnormal and Social Psychology*, 35:4-10, 11-16,

Since the real curative agent in mental disease is love in its various forms, this explains why many eminent apostles of love have been able to cure mental disorders of legions of persons, though these altruists did not have any special psychiatric training. Their sublime love and supraconscious wisdom have been an excellent substitute for "the little or no love" and the professional training of the ordinary psychiatrists. It is true that for a successful cure of especially serious mental disorders a mere blind-subconscious love and too-dried-up "intellectualized" love is not enough. Unwise, "inadequate," and blind love of mother sometimes spoils the child or the recipient of such a love. Elsewhere it has been pointed out that the truly creative and curative love must be not only pure and intensive but also "adequate" or wise, choosing the adequate means for the realization of its supreme objective. Otherwise, it may miscarry and harm rather than benefit and cure.[70] The need and important role of an adequate scientific training is not canceled by the thesis that love is the main agent. To do its work effectively, it needs to be competently guided, channeled, and used. In geniuses their supraconscious supplies this guidance. For the ordinary therapists their scientific training performs this function.[71] Stressing the importance of either supraconscious or scientific guidance of love, the curative power

---

1940; W. U. Snyder, "An Investigation of the Nature of Non-Directive Therapy," *Journal of General Psychology*, 33:193-223, 1945.
[70] Cf. P. Sorokin, "Love and Its Aspects," *Explorations*, quoted, p. 27 ff.
[71] Cf. on this I. N. Korner, "Ego Involvement and the Process of Disengagement," *Journal of Consulting Psychology*, 14:206-209, 1950; W. Seeman, "Clinical Opinion on the Role of Therapist Adjustment in Psychotherapy," *Journal of Consulting Psychology*, 14:49-52, 1950.

of love remains indispensable for practically all successful therapeutic treatments of mental disorders.

6. LOVE AS THE MAINSPRING OF LIFE AND OF LIFE EVOLUTION

The discussed curative and life-giving functions of love follow from the very nature of love as the concentrated form of life and from the nature of life as a form of love-energy. This conception of life has been well outlined by Ashley Montagu,[72] and can also be summed up as follows:

"The biological counterpart of love-energy manifests itself in the very nature and basic processes of life. This energy, still little known, and often called the 'vital energy' that mysteriously unites various inorganic energies into a startling unity of a living—unicellular or multicellular—organism, is the first biological manifestation of the Empedoclean energy of love. The generation of practically all unicellular organisms from a parent cell, either by fission of the parent cell into four new individuals (zoöspores) or into thirty-two or sixty-four microzoöids with a subsequent conjugation of gametes into a new organism, is another manifestation of 'biological love-energy'. . . . The two are for a time bound together in an interactive association. . . . The life of either one or the other is at some time dependent upon the potential or actual being of the other. Without such an interaction—without the parent cell supplying the vital tissues to the new organism, and without metabolic and physiological exchanges between parent and daughter cells —the appearance of a new organism is impossible; the very continuity of life itself becomes impossible. Cooperation of two organisms in sexual reproduction of multicellular organisms, accompanied by the passion of biological attraction between

[72] Cf. Ashley Montagu, *On Being Human* (New York, 1950). See there the details, the evidence, and the main literature.

them, is a visible form of this 'biological love' necessary for the maintenance of all such species and, through that, of life itself. The parental care of the offspring, during its period of helplessness, the care that in some species like *Homo sapiens* must last several years, is a still more explicit manifestation of biological love-energy. Without it such species would die out. A diverse cooperation and mutual aid functioning practically among all the species and necessary for their survival is a still more explicit and universal manifestation of biological love-energy. This cooperation, mutual aid, 'gregarious or social instinct,' 'empathy,' 'sympathy,' are rightly considered a 'fundamental characteristic of life-phenomena' as universal and basic as the trait of the 'struggle for existence.' " [73]

"The 'cooperative forces are biologically the more important and vital [than the antagonizing forces]. The balance between the cooperative, altruistic tendencies and those which are disoperative and egoistic is relatively close [in biological organisms]. In the long run, however, the group-centered, more altruistic drives are slightly stronger—such is the summary of this situation.'[74]

[73] P. Sorokin, "Love; Its Aspects," *Explorations*, quoted, pp. 16-17. See also Peter Kropotkin, *Mutual Aid* (London, 1902); W. C. Allee, *Animal Aggregations* (Chicago, 1931); *The Social Life of Animals* (New York, 1938); E. F. Darling, *Bird Flocks and the Breeding Cycle* (Cambridge, 1938); A. E. Emerson, "The Biological Basis of Social Cooperation," *Illinois Academy of Science Transactions*, Vol. XXXIX, 1946; R. Gerard, "Higher Level of Integration," in *Biological Symposia*, Vol. VIII, 1942; R. S. Little, *General Biology and Philosophy of Organism* (Chicago, 1945); S. J. Holmes, *Life and Morals* (New York, 1948); Ashley Montagu, *op. cit., passim;* Charles Sherrington, *Man on His Nature* (New York, 1941); Sri Aurobindo, *The Life Divine* (New York, 1949).

[74] W. C. Allee, "Where Angels Fear to Tread," *Science*, Vol. XCVII, 1943, pp. 518-25. See other considerations and facts in Ashley Montagu's and other cited works.

"To sum up: without the operation of a biological counterpart of love-energy life itself is not possible, nor its continuity, nor the preservation and survival of species, nor life evolution, nor the emergence and evolution of *Homo sapiens*. Without uniting, integrating, and coordinating functions of biological love-energy the world of life could have hardly emerged, and after its emergence it would certainly have perished in the war of anything living with anything living, in the incessant universal struggle for existence of each living unit with the rest of the organic and inorganic universe."[75]

"An enormous body of evidence has been produced showing that the principle of cooperation has possibly been even more important in the evolutionary process than that of the egoistic struggle for existence. From the simplest protozoa up to man, mutual aid in various forms is found to function among all species, especially among those that have to nurture their offspring. For man mutual aid has been the condition of survival of the species. Owing to its helplessness, a newly born child has to be taken care of for a number of years. The very biological interdependence of the two sexes of *Homo sapiens* dictates their living together, their cooperation and mutual aid. Before human culture and weapons were developed, men could defend themselves against stronger species and many destructive forces only by living together, in groups with coordinated collective activities." [76]

This basic fact of love's being the mainspring of life itself explains the life-giving, life-sustaining, and curative powers of love as well as the decisive role of love and cooperation in the evolution of life itself.

---

[75] P. Sorokin, "Love: Its Aspects," *Explorations,* quoted, pp. 16-17.
[76] P. Sorokin, *Reconstruction of Humanity* (Boston, 1948), pp. 67-68.

7. THE CREATIVE AND INTEGRATIVE POWER OF LOVE IN THE LIFE OF AN INDIVIDUAL

Love not only cures and revitalizes the individual's mind and organism. It proves itself as the decisive factor of vital, mental, moral, and social well-being and growth of an individual. The unwanted, unloved, "rejected" babies, deprived of the grace of love at an early age, tend to die or to grow into distorted, unhappy, uncreative, deficient and delinquent "human plants." They are like seedlings planted in an unfertile soil and deprived of the necessary ingredients for their normal growth and activity. If in these conditions such seedlings do not die, they grow stunted, misshapen, weak, and ugly. Babies and children not blessed by the grace of love of their family, playmates, and neighbors grow into unhappy, defective, and often delinquent, human beings. To love and be loved turns out to be the most important "vitamin," indispensable for a sound growth of an individual and a happy course of human life.

This is well corroborated by two opposite sets of evidence. On the one hand, children unloved, unwanted and "rejected" by their parents, siblings, and others, yield a much higher quota of juvenile delinquents, adult criminals, physically and mentally defective persons than the children adequately loved by the members of their family, playmates, and by others. Unloved and unloving children produce a higher rate of warped, hostile, and unbalanced persons than the children blessed by the grace of love. The evidence supporting this generalization is substantial and adequate.[77] On the other hand, almost all of

[77] Cf. A. Montagu, *On Being Human* (New York, 1950); M. Merrill, *Problems of Child Delinquency* (New York, 1947); H. Witmer, "The

those Christian Saints who quietly, without any tragedy and sudden conversion, grew into apostles of love came from harmonious families where they were wanted and loved.[78]

Of 500 living American Good Neighbors, 70.6 percent had a very happy and 18 percent a fairly happy childhood, with loving and understanding parents and with an atmosphere of love prevalent in the family. The overwhelming majority of these good neighbors have their own families also well integrated, harmonious, and blessed by the grace of love.[79]

Of 484 Harvard and Radcliffe students investigated, of those who had a happy childhood and were loved in their family, 67 percent view the world and fellow men affiliatively, and 20 percent with hostility; of those who had an unhappy childhood and were loved little only 50 percent are affiliative and 27 percent are hostile to others and the world at large.[80]

The positive and negative sets of facts well confirm

Outcome of Treatment in a Child Guidance Clinic," *Smith College in Social Work*, v. 3, 1933; W. Warren, "Conduct Disorders in Children," *British Journal of Delinquency*, 1:164-186, 1951; C. Burt, *The Young Delinquent* (London, 1925); E. Shilder, "Family Disintegration and the Boy Delinquent," *Journal of Criminal Law and Criminology*, 8:709-732, 1918; W. A. Lunden, *Juvenile Delinquency* (Pittsburgh, 1936); S. and E. Glueck, *Unraveling Juvenile Delinquency* (New York, 1950).

[78] Cf. P. Sorokin, *Altruistic Love* (Boston, 1950), pp. 136-37, 245.
[79] *Ibid.*, pp. 25-28, 30-32.
[80] P. Sorokin, "Affiliative and Hostile Tendencies of College Students," *Explorations in Altruistic Love and Behavior* (Boston, 1950); W. D. Wall, "Happiness and Unhappiness in Childhood and Adolescence," *British Journal of Psychology*, 38:191-208, 1948.

that the grace of love is indispensable in forming the sound, integrated, and creative personality. This constructive function of love is one of its many forms of power.

8. LOVE AS CREATIVE POWER IN SOCIAL MOVEMENTS

With the exception of the reference to love as the mainspring of life and of biological evolution, we have dealt so far mainly with the influence of love upon individuals and interindividual relationships. Fortunately, the power of love is not limited by this influence. It goes far beyond individual relationships and cases. It affects the whole ocean of social and cultural life of humanity. It operates as the driving force of mankind's creative progress toward ever fuller Truth, ever nobler Goodness, ever purer Beauty, ever richer Freedom, and ever finer forms of social life and institutions. Throughout human history each positive step in this direction has been inspired and "powered" by love, while any regressive step away from these values has been driven by hate.

Let us begin by a few cases of the influence of love upon vast social movements. We can start with concrete questions: can the non-violent power of love stop war and give peace? Can the peaceful power of love achieve important social reforms and constructive changes? Can it compete with the social reconstructions inspired by hate and carried on by the means of violent and bloody struggle?

A number of clear-cut historical events give an answer to these questions. As a first case of the power of love in regard to war and peace, Asoka's experiment may be mentioned. After his accession to the throne in 273 B.C., Asoka, like his predecessors, spent the first twelve years of his reign in wars of consolidation of his Indian empire.

The conquest of the province of Kalinga in 261 B.C. was his last war. From Asoka's own inscriptions we learn that the horrors and miseries of war aroused in him a deep remorse, a sense of profoundest shame, and an understanding of the utter futility of war as the means of pacification and of social improvement. As a result, in 261-260 B.C., he was converted to Buddhism, as a lay-disciple, and in 259, he entered the Buddhist Order as a monk. This date marks a complete transformation of Asoka and of his policies. The successful emperor-warrior changed into a zealous apostle of peace, compassion, love, and good works. He began now to preach, to practice, and to carry on "the policies of goodness, mercy, liberality, truthfulness, purity, and gentleness," especially toward the conquered peoples, and the policies of liberation from "depravity, violence, cruelty, anger, conceit, and envy." Specific duties required from his followers and officials were: non-slaughter of animate beings, non-injury to "existing creatures"; hearkening to father and mother; reverence to teachers; liberality and seemly behavior toward friends, acquaintances, fellow men, and ascetics; compassionate and seemly conduct toward slaves and servants; and "small expense and small accumulation."

His works of charity consisted in planting the roads with shade trees and orchards, building rest houses and watering sheds, and in digging wells; in constructing hospitals and dispensaries (for men and animals); in distributing medical drugs; in planting medicinal herbs and fruit trees; in outright grants of money and organized relief to the poor, the aged, the helpless, the prisoners, the infirm, and needy people generally.

His *political administration* was marked by complete

cessation of wars and the establishment of undisturbed peace—internal and external; by the establishment of a special class of high officials (*Dharma-Mahamatras*) whose duties were concerned solely with the temporal and spiritual welfare of the people. *All* his political officers were to follow Asoka's example in their personal behavior. They were exhorted to carry on the policy of good will, sympathy, and love toward their own people, as well as toward the peoples of the bordering territories. The officials were missionaries and moral leaders. One of their main functions was to be "the peacemakers" between all sects, races, parties, and peoples, building their mutual good will and decreasing their enmities. Asoka revised the existing laws and judicial administration, making these more just, humane, and uniform. He made himself available for the business of the people at any and all times.

Asoka's *cultural activities* resulted in spreading mental and moral education among the people; in stimulating the fine arts, particularly the art of the theatre. The amphitheatres were used, among other things, to dramatize the enjoyments which would follow from a life of virtue, the improvement in the economic conditions of the people, and the like.

To sum up: here we have a striking example of a peaceful, love-motivated social, mental, moral, and aesthetic reconstruction of an empire.[81] Was Asoka's experiment successful? It certainly was. He secured internal and external peace in his Empire not only up to his death in 232 B.C. but for an additional 30 to 40 years after his

---

[81] See the details of the life and activities of Asoka in D. R. Bhandarkar, *Asoka* (Calcutta, 1932); V. A. Smith, *Asoka, the Buddhist Emperor of India* (Oxford, 1909).

death, that is, for the period of some 60 to 70 years. A systematic study of all the wars in the history of Greece, Rome, Austria, Germany, the Netherlands, Spain, Italy, France, England, Russia, Poland, and Lithuania from 600 B.C. up to the present time shows that out of each 100 years of their history they were involved in war from 28 to 67 years. In other words, these countries had on the average a war in every two to four years of their history.

"This does not mean that the years of war and peace in the history of any country have been evenly distributed; some periods had uninterrupted war during two, five, ten, or thirty, and so on, years; other periods have had several years of undisturbed peace. But periods of peace as long as one quarter of a century have been exceedingly rare in the history of all countries, and a period up to 100 years or more of peace is almost unique, given in the history of Holland; in some of these countries long periods of peace did not occur at all. Almost every generation (25 to 30 years) in the past, with very few exceptions, has been a witness of, or an actor in, war phenomena." [82]

In the light of these data the period of uninterrupted peace for some 60 to 70 years achieved by the love-inspired, non-violent, peaceful policy of Asoka is thus an exceptionally rare achievement in the history of all countries at all times. It is the policy radically opposed to the Roman policy of *si vis pacem para bellum* ("if you want peace, prepare for war"), or to its contemporary version of "peace through armed power."

From the remotest past to the present time this preda-

[82] P. Sorokin, *Social and Cultural Dynamics* (New York, 1937), v. III, p. 352. See there a systematic study of all the wars and of the periods of peace in the history of the countries mentioned from 600 B.C. up to 1925 A.D.

tory policy of "peace through armed power," intimidation, coercion, and destruction has been followed by an overwhelming majority of governments of all countries. In spite of its past and present glorification, in spite of an endless repetition of this "enmity-fueled" policy, it has given neither lasting peace to humanity, nor has it yielded even relatively long peaceful periods in the history of practically any country. After innumerable applications of this predatory and hate-loaded policy for millennia, twentieth-century mankind finds itself in the bloodiest, most warlike, most inhuman, and most destructive century of the twenty-five preceding centuries studied.[83]

A detailed study of war and peace periods in the history of the above-mentioned twelve countries shows that an overwhelming majority of the relatively long peaceful periods of some fifteen years and over occurred at times when the ruling groups and the people of the respective countries were neither ambitious for military glory nor believed much in sheer force of arms, nor were anxious to conquer their neighbors, nor hated other countries. If anything, like the governments and people of the Netherlands during the nineteenth and the beginning of the twentieth century, when that country had a century of peace; or like the governments and peoples of Switzerland and Belgium during their long neutrality period, the ruling groups during the long periods of peace were more humanitarian and peace-aspiring than the carnivorous, war-intoxicated and conquest-inspired ruling groups of the long war-periods. In other words, comparatively long

[83] Cf. for the actual data on the movement of wars in the last twenty-five centuries and for the evidence of the twentieth century's being the bloodiest of all these centuries, *ibid.,* pp. 259-382.

periods of peace are closely correlated with peace-aspiring and humanitarian governments, whereas the long periods of war are associated with militant and hate-inspired expansionists and domineering governments, trusting mainly the power of arms, coercion, and destruction of the enemy.[84]

In the light of these statements the extraordinary success of Asoka's policy of peace and love is not accidental but is a conspicuous case of a fairly general pattern. *In the internal and external policies of nations and empires, love also begets love and hate produces hate.* It is highly regrettable that our statesmen, diplomats, and contemporary ruling groups still transgress this rule, believing still in peace through the power of limitless arming, unbounded hate, and pitiless crushing of the actual or potential enemy. No wonder they have utterly failed in establishing peace and strikingly succeeded only in starting and expanding the bloodiest, the most terrible, the most inhuman, and the most destructive wars in all of human history. Their policies well demonstrate the truth that hate produces hate, physical force and war beget counter-force and counter-war, and rarely, if ever, do these factors lead to peace and social well-being.

Asoka's policy was highly successful also internally. Without any violence and bloodshed it fruitfully carried on one of the greatest social, economic, political, legal, mental, moral, spiritual, and aesthetic reconstructions of empire in the whole history of humanity. For its time and for all time, Asoka's reconstruction was deeper, greater, and more constructive than any reconstruction done

[84] Cf. for all such periods, Sorokin's *Dynamics,* quoted, v. III, pp. 259-380.

through bloody revolutions and violence. Again the success of Asoka's internal policy was not accidental. It was but a conspicuous case of a fairly general pattern that *the love-inspired reconstructions, aspiring for real well-being of the people, and carried out in a peaceful manner, are more successful and yield more lasting positive results than the social reconstructions inspired by hate and carried out mainly by violence and bloodshed.* Though in our Sensate age of violence and bloodshed this truth is entirely ignored, it still remains an unshaken truth. Besides the peaceful reforms and bloody revolutions of the past, the events of our age convincingly prove its validity. They prove it positively and negatively. The unlimited violence and the hate-inspired war policies of the First World War, of the Second World War, of the Korean war and of the Chinese, the Russian, the Fascist, and the Hitler Revolutions strikingly demonstrate the utter futility of the hate-driven wars and revolutions in improving the total well-being of humanity. First of all, the empires quickly built by unlimited war and violence, such as the empires of Alexander the Great, Caesar, Genghis Khan, Tamerlane, Suleiman the Magnificent, and Napoleon—up to the quickly expanded empires of Japan in 1941-1945, Hitler, Mussolini—all such empires crumbled within a few years or decades after their establishment. Within one decade the empires of Japan, Hitler, and Mussolini enormously expanded and shrank to limits smaller than they were before the expansion.

The two world wars aimed to improve the welfare of mankind and to make the world safe for democracy and freedom. Instead, they destroyed about one-sixth of the most inhabited regions of this planet, killed and wounded more than a hundred million human beings, brought misery, disease, and poverty to the greater part of humanity, blew to pieces all the finest values, spread insanity and demoralization, unleashed in man "the worst of the beasts," and created an unprecedented chaos and anarchy. Instead of freedom and democracy, they have given unlimited tyranny, autocracy, totalitarianism, and universal coercion. The Korean war has utterly ruined a country of some thirty million people and has already killed from five to ten million innocent Koreans. The net balance of these wars is quite negative: they greatly decrease the vital, mental, moral, social, and economic well-being of humanity. For all persons who have open eyes and sound minds, this conclusion is inescapable.

The same may be said of the recent Chinese, Russian, Fascist, Nazi, and other lesser revolutions. The Chinese Revolution was started in 1911 and is still continuing with unabated strength. The net result of some forty years of this revolution is millions of victims, untold suffering and bestiality, and a notably lower level of the total well-being of the Chinese nation in comparison with the pre-revolutionary level. Almost all the loudly advertised "achievements" of the Revolution remain mainly "paper achievements," "empty shells," without real value-content. The negative balance of the Fascist and the Nazi revolutions is evident: their boasted "conquests" vanished quickly and so did all their temporary triumphs. Millions of killed and wounded human derelicts, destruction, and misery are all that remain from their "achievements." The net balance of the Russian Revolution is similar. In spite of some twenty million direct victims of the Revolution; in spite of some twenty million indirect casualties;

notwithstanding all the boastful "five-year plans" and all the Soviet propaganda "successes" of the Revolution, the Russian nation has now a more tyrannical regime than the Czarist regime at its worst; the economic well-being is still lower than it was before 1914; the creative work of the nation is less exuberant in most fields of culture than it was before the Revolution; the moral and mental well-being of the Russian people is hardly higher now than it was before the Revolution. Of course, pitilessly exploiting the great nation, the Soviet regime could not help achieving a few positive results, but these results look modest in comparison with those that were peacefully achieved before the Revolution, and those which would have been achieved if the Revolution had not occurred.[85]

The evidence of these wars and revolutions is well confirmed by the wars and revolutions of the past. Beginning with the oldest recorded Egyptian revolution *circa* 3000 B.C., up to the recent revolutions, they all testify to the utter futility of hate-driven mass-violence as a means of realizing the well-being of mankind. If some positive ef-

---

[85] Cf. for the full evidence of the statements on the sterility and destruction of war-built empires and bloody, hate-inspired revolutions, P. Sorokin, *Sociology of Revolution* (Philadelphia, 1924); *Leaves from a Russian Diary*, 2nd ed. (Boston, 1950); the essay: "Thirty Years After," *Social and Cultural Dynamics*, v. III, pp. 383-508, which gives so far the only existing study of all the revolutions and important internal disturbances from 600 B.C. up to 1925 A.D., in the history of Greece, Rome, Byzantium, France, Germany, Austria, England, Italy, Spain, the Netherlands, Russia, Poland, Lithuania. See also *S.O.S.: The Meaning of Our Crisis* (Boston, 1951); and *Man and Society in Calamity* (New York, 1942). In these works a vast body of factual evidence is given in favor of the summary statements in this paper.

fects are achieved by these movements, they are due mainly to the stream of love, compassion, sympathy, and sincere desire to help the exploited masses that is ever present even within these movements, and that alone achieves some good results amid the prevalent hate-ridden destructive forces of wars and revolutions. Even among the violent revolutions themselves, the more hate-driven, the more bloody and destructive the revolution, the less fruitful and lasting are its constructive results.

The negative evidence of wars and bloody revolutions is confirmed by the fruitfulness of humanitarian, peaceful, and love-inspired, orderly social reconstructions.

The recent reorganization of India may serve as a modern example of such reconstruction. It was begun and carried on under the leadership of Mahatma Gandhi and his co-workers. Their policy has been motivated by creative love at its purest and best. Hate and enmity have been explicitly ruled out from their movement. So also have any violent means and methods. Throughout its whole history the Gandhi-led movement has been peaceful and orderly. Its constructive results have been truly astounding. It has achieved a complete political independence for India and for some 400 millions of people. This result alone exceeds the political achievements of practically any violent revolution known in human history. Gandhi's movement succeeded in liberating and giving equality to some 60 million outcasts in India—another result hardly rivaled by any "liberation" of any violent revolution. The peaceful crusade of Gandhi and his co-workers in this movement has already achieved a most significant amelioration of vital, economic, mental, moral, and cultural conditions of the vast population of India. Besides the inestimably fruitful reconstruction of India, it has produced tremendous reverberations in the whole human universe. The entire world has been constructively affected by Gandhi's policy and by its results. It has convincingly shown the boundless effectiveness of the policy of love, sympathy, and good will carried on by non-violent means, without hate and inhuman destruction. If all its positive results are summed up, they unquestionably surpass the constructive results of any violent revolution or war. India's modern reconstruction is an eloquent demonstration of the gigantic power of love in the truly creative rebuilding of a vast nation and its potential for the whole of mankind.

This power of love continues to work in India not only in the policies of the successors of Gandhi in the present government of India, but in hundreds of other movements, private and public. The activities of "the holy man," Acharya Vinoba Bhave, who is one of the disciples of Gandhi, are an example of these "smaller" movements. Practicing the principles of love he preaches, this gentle ascetic, by merely appealing to the goodness of human nature, in his "one-man crusade" has already achieved astounding results. His speeches on non-violence as the only fruitful way of solution of economic and social problems have won thousands of oppressed peasants away from Communism, and have convinced many a landlord freely to give up a part of his land to the needy cultivators. "Single-handed, he attacked India's grave land problem, which is the source of rural unrest, and swiftly brought about the redistribution of 35,000 acres of land by landlords to their tenants, without coercion or the payment of an *anna*. . . . The Central Ministry of Food and Agrire has been sufficiently impressed with his methods to ːr 10,000,000 acres of Government-owned cultivable ˌasteland for him to distribute, personally, among the landless."[86] His goal is 50,000,000 acres—one-sixth of the total cultivable land of India—to be freely given by landlords for distribution among the landless and the needy.

The fruitfulness of social reforms inspired by love rather than by hate, carried on peacefully rather than by bloodshed and violence, is demonstrated by practically all such reconstructions in the history of various countries. "The Great Reforms" of 1861-65 in Russia that liberated serfs and basically reorganized political, social, economic, and cultural institutions were another highly successful peaceful reconstruction. The westernization of Japan and the basic reorganization of its institutions, carried on in orderly fashion during the second half of the nineteenth and at the beginning of the twentieth centuries, is another successful reconstruction. Its positive success becomes especially clear when it is contrasted with Japan's violent experiments to reconstruct herself and Asia as the "co-prosperity area." Starting with the Pearl Harbor attack, this "reconstruction," carried on by means of unlimited bloodshed, resulted in a catastrophic self-destruction of Japan and in deadly devastation of China and other Asian countries. It has shown indeed that "it does not pay to be violent and destructive."

The reason for this contrast is at hand. After all, violent, hate-inspired, destructive revolutions and wars are but a form of "social sickness" similar to the sickness of an organism. As long as all parts of an organism cooperate

[86] Cf. R. Trumbull, "Holy Man Who Walks in Gandhi's Step," *New York Times,* Magazine Section, February 10, 1952, pp. 13, 30.

harmoniously and maintain their inner and external equilibrium, the organism lives a healthy life and is free from sickness. When the harmonious cooperation of the parts of the organism with one another and of the organism with its milieu is broken, it becomes sick. Sickness means the breakdown of the internal and external cooperation of the life-forces of the organism. This sickness can only be cured by the life-forces. A successful cure of sickness cannot be achieved by mere application of bloody, hateful, and violent means. Instead, a scientifically competent, orderly, and sympathy-inspired therapy is needed. When an operation is prescribed, it must be an operation by a competent surgeon and aimed at the recovery of the sick, but not a violent and hate-inspired butchery. In the application to an organism these platitudes are well known and understood by all.

In regard to "social sickness" this understanding is still lacking. As long as the members of a given society or of a universe of societies cooperate with one another, the societies live a peaceful and harmonious life. When the cooperation, with underlying mutual sympathy and tolerance dries up, the social tensions, enmities, and antagonisms emerge. Society or the universe of societies becomes "sick." Social sickness generates social suffering, fever, and social movements. Intentionally or not, the movements aim to get rid of the sickness. As in biological illness, a mere violence and blind bloodshed are not enough to effect the cure of social sickness. Scientific competence and sincere love for the patient are no less necessary here than in medical illness. If even "a social operation" is in order, it must be aimed at curing the patient, not at killing him. In medical as in social operations, hate-laden, blind butchery harms rather than cures, kills rather than revives, destroys rather than builds. If anything good comes of such wars and revolutions, it is due to the current of unselfish love and disinterested desire to help the suffering multitudes but not to hate and blind destruction. In addition, most of the positive results of such violent movements are obtained through spoliation of some other groups, at the cost of their suffering, their well-being, often, their very life. Most of the "achievements" of bloody wars and revolutions are a mere spoliation of the defeated party by the victorious group. A mere transfer of goods from one "ruling gang" to another does not enrich the whole society, nor does it increase the total sum of the goods; it does not eliminate mutual hates, antagonisms, and injustices, nor does it cure, indeed, the social sickness. It merely changes the ruling actors and the forms of tyranny, exploitation, misery, injustice, hate, and tensions, without a notable decrease in the total fund of social evils.

While the victorious ruling faction profits by war or violent revolution, the bulk of the populations of both struggling parties must bear the cost of the struggle. And the bloodier the struggle, the greater the cost—in life, property, and happiness for the broad masses. In protracted and bloody struggles, the vital, economic, mental, and moral losses of vast strata of both parties ordinarily far exceed their gains. While small ruling groups or individuals such as Ghengis Khan, Napoleon, Marius, Sulla, Caesar, Antony, Cromwell, Robespierre, Lenin, or Hitler for a short time enormously profited by their victories, the vast multitude of their peoples was virtually ruined by the struggle. Sometimes the ruin was irreparable and eventually led to the decline of the bled nations and of their cultural creativity. Bloody civil strifes and the Peloponnesian War ushered in the decay of Greece; the costly wars and the bloodiest civil strifes of Marius and Sulla, of the First and the Second Triumvirates, started the decline of the Roman Empire. The bloodshed of the French Revolution and of the Napoleonic wars prepared the subsequent eclipse of France. The same can be said of the wars of Suleiman the Magnificent in regard to the Turkish Empire or of the decay of the Old Kingdom, the Middle, and the New Empire in Egypt. Finally, the bloodiest revolutions and the world wars of our time have brought all of mankind, especially the belligerent and turbulent West (including Russia), to the brink of an apocalyptic catastrophe. The hate-inspired, predatory, blind, and bloody butcheries do not improve social well-being; neither do they cure social illness. Only wisely guided forces of love and free cooperation can perform these functions. Where they are lacking, no constructive results for the whole of humanity can be expected.

9. LOVE AS THE SUPREME AND VITAL FORM OF
HUMAN RELATIONSHIP

Human relations of interacting individuals to one another can be *compulsory,* like the relationship of master and slave, of executioner and executed, of prisoner and guard, of victim and victor. Or the ties binding the individuals into a group can be *contractual,* each party trying freely to get from the other parties as much advantage as possible for as little as possible, as in the relationship between buyer and seller, "free" employee and employer, "free" prostitute and her customer. Or the social bonds can consist of a *love-relationship* sought and aspired to for its own sake. In love-relationship the egos of the parties are freely merged into one "we"; joys and sorrows of one party are joys and sorrows of the other (s); the ego of one person is fully identified with that of the other (s); if separated, the parties feel unhappy and spontaneously try to be together. Their mutual love is the end-value for them. Each party gladly does and gives anything for the well-being of the other party. There is no bargain nor calculation of profits, pleasures, and utilities. The relationship between the loving mother and her child, between a truly loving husband and wife, true friends, and between all those who practice the love-precepts of the Sermon on the Mount are examples of love-relationship.

It goes without saying that the finest, the noblest, and the happiest human society is the society of individuals bound together by love-relationship. It is the freest society because the very meaning of "I love to be here," or "I love to do this," or "I love to be a member" is the highest expression of the free desire, action, and preference of a person. It is the happiest society because loving and being loved is the highest form of happiness in human relationship. It is the most peaceful and harmonious society. It is also the most creative, most beautiful, and noblest.

Love-relationship is not only the best; its minimum is absolutely necessary for a long and enjoyable existence of human society and social life generally. A society bound together only by coercive bonds is but the worst prison society, permeated by mutual hate, deprived of any freedom, joyless and drab. Prisoners always try to escape from it. It is a social hell hardly worth living in. If mankind were destined to live in such a universal prison, neither mankind nor its social life could survive.

Contractual society is much better than the prison society, but when completely deprived of love-relationship, it too cannot successfully survive for a long time. Fully egoistic individuals contractually taking advantage of one another soon will find themselves engaged in a merciless struggle for existence, in a mutual "cold" and "hot" war, into a Hobbesian *bellum omnium contra omnes*. In unlimited free competition stronger individuals soon will be "freely" exploiting and subjugating the weaker ones; society soon will be divided into the rich and the poor, the aristocracy and the plebs, the victors and the victims, the masters and the serfs, with mutual hatred and inevitable degeneration into a compulsory type of society. Only the "strands of love-relationship" interwoven into the bulk of contractual relationships warm the otherwise cold contractual society, moderate its unlimited struggle for existence, and prevent it from turning into a compulsory prison with frequent riots and "civil wars" of the prison population. In addition, if the relationships of the members of the competitive-contractual society were fully deprived of love-relationships, if the members did not love anyone and were not loved, the incessant free-for-all struggle for existence would soon become tiresome, joyless, and senseless. Bargaining for the sake of bargaining, merciless cutthroat rivalry for the sake of rivalry is not an end-value that can be continued for its own sake forever. It has some sense and value only when the bargainers love somebody and want to help them, or want to use the accumulated means for higher ends, which always contain love for something or somebody and concern for the well-being of other human beings.

If at the present time the Western "capitalist-contractual Society" is crumbling in the conflagration of multitudinous hates, strifes, and wars, one of the reasons for it is exactly the lack of the necessary minimum of love-relationship. Through this lack, its unlimited rivalry has degenerated into an unlimited "war of everyone with everyone," and its free contractual relationships have turned in ever-increasing measure into compulsory ones.

Only a notable infusion of love-relationship into this society can save it from its further degeneration into either compulsory-totalitarian society or into chaotic human flotsam.

To sum up: love-relationship is not only the supreme form of social relationship, it is an absolute necessity for a harmonious existence and survival of any social group. Without it no good social life is possible. Plato and Aristotle were quite right in their statement that friendship or love is the most vital stuff of all true social relationships. Often overlooked, this function of love shows its unique power in the social life of man and in man's historical process.[87]

10. LOVE-POWER IN KNOWLEDGE, BEAUTY, GOODNESS, FREEDOM, AND HAPPINESS

Finally, love furnishes a considerable driving force to the total power of each of the highest values of human life: to the power of truth and knowledge, of beauty, freedom,

[87] Cf. on this P. Sorokin, *Society, Culture, and Personality,* chaps. 5, 6, 7.

goodness, and happiness. Each of these end-values has its own power that tangibly affects, enriches, and ennobles the life of individuals, groups, and the course of human history. Entering as a component into each of these values, love adds a considerable driving force to their own power. Thus *love of truth* makes the search for truth more forceful, enjoyable, and indefatigable than a pursuit of truth either coercively imposed or contractually stipulated. Most of the valid truths of humanity have been discovered through the love of truth rather than through coercion or contractual obligation. Love of truth not only stimulates scientific discoveries, inventions, philosophical and religious verities, but *love directly* contributes to our knowledge and learning. Through empathy and communion, coparticipation in the experience of all who are loved, love enormously enriches our poor individual experience. When love embraces the whole of humanity, one becomes coparticipant in the richest experience of all generations. This empathic, sympathetic, loving way of learning is possibly one of the surest and most efficient methods of cognition and the most fruitful way to truth and knowledge. In this sense love-experience leads to a true cognition, and love transforms itself into truth and knowledge.[88] In these two ways the power of love greatly reinforces the power of truth and knowledge.

Similarly, love greatly increases the *power of beauty*. *Love of beauty* is a precondition of all the innumerable ac-

[88] Like the transformation of physical energies of heat, motion, electricity, etc., into one another, the energies of love, truth, beauty, etc., are also transformable into one another. Cf. on this P. Sorokin, "Love: Its Aspects," in *Explorations*, quoted, pp. 20-21, 29-30.

tions of aspiration, creation, and enjoyment of all that is beautiful in human life, in the fine arts, and in human history. In a sense love is beauty's indispensable component. Anything that one loves and looks at through loving eyes becomes "lovely," that is, beautiful. Anything unloved appears "unlovely," often ugly. Since the love-experience is beautiful in its very nature, everything that love touches becomes beautiful. Love immortalizes the mortal, ennobles the ignoble, beautifies the ugly, and makes the whole world a beautiful place to live. Love generates the search for beauty and supplies an immense driving power to the energy of beauty itself. Through the factor of beauty love notably affects our life and the course of history. Love-power has been working in and is embodied in all phenomena of the arts, beginning with the enjoyment of a sunset and the beauty of the beloved, and ending with Homer's epic and Shakespeare's tragedy, Beethoven's and Bach's music, Michelangelo's sculpture, the Parthenon, and the Cathedral of Chartres.

Likewise, *love for freedom* has been instrumental in all the innumerable actions and movements for realization of freedom in human history. Even more: love-experience is freedom at its loftiest and best. To love anything is to act freely, without compulsion or artificial stimulation. To be free means to do what one loves to do. In this sense, love and true freedom are synonymous. Compulsion is the negation of love. Where there is love, there is no coercion: where there is coercion, there is no love. And the greater the love, the greater the freedom. A person who loves all humanity is free in the human universe; a person who loves the whole world is free in the whole cosmos. A persons who hates the world is the greatest of slaves—objectively and subjectively. Anything and anybody is his enemy; everything hinders him, opposes him, and limits his freedom in every action, thought, and volition. Without love all the bills of rights and all the constitutional guarantees of freedom are but empty shells.

There is no need to argue that *love is the heart and soul of ethical goodness itself and of all great religions.* Their central command has always been love of God and of neighbor. Their main verity is "God is Love and Love is God." Without love there is no morality and no religion. If the stream of love in religion or ethics dries up, both become empty and dead.

Finally, *love-experience is the supreme form of happiness.* Love contributes to it in many ways. First of all as the most powerful antidote against fear and insecurity. Love "beareth all things, endureth all things . . . never faileth." Love does not fear anything or anybody. It cuts off the very roots of fear. Where there is fear, there is no love; where there is love, there is no fear. Fear comes from a selfish idea of cutting one's ego off from the universe. The smaller and the more selfish a person's ego, the greater his fear. He trembles at any infringement of his puniest possessions and worthless idiosyncrasies. Love transcends our ego; it identifies our Self with the Infinite Reality-Value. Such a Self is not afraid of anything or anybody. The best and most scientific remedy against fear is boundless love. Without love there is no remedy for this disease. With love there is no fear, no trembling and no insecurity.

Disarming fear, love contributes to our happiness by

blessing us with the *highest peace of mind*. Neither the puny "peace of mind" of Freudians, nor the lollipop "peace of mind" of best-sellers on "how to stop worrying" can give us a real peace of mind. Only all-embracing and all-forgiving love that "suffereth long, seeketh not her own" brings an indestructible tranquility of mind. When love is slight and impure, its peace of mind is impure and vulnerable. When it is unbounded and pure, it is "the peace of God that passeth all understanding."

Finally, the experience of a truly great love is the highest form of happiness itself. It is the *summum bonum*. Each experience of loving and being loved, however simple and impure, is already a happy experience, "a moment of sunshine" in our grayish life process. An experience of a great love is the highest bliss of human life. And vice versa. Any life deprived of love is a mere miserable existence. Such a life often becomes unbearable and leads its victims to suicide.

Thus the power of love generates, inspires, reinforces, and operates in all the individual and collective actions of realization of Truth and Knowledge, of Goodness and Justice, of Beauty and Freedom, of the *Summum Bonum* and Happiness throughout the whole creative history of humanity. When all the forms of manifestation of love-power are rightly understood, one can but agree with Gandhi's and Dostoievsky's re-statements of the old truth on the power of love.

A real apostle of love "will yield an influence greater than that of the sceptred monarch," correctly says Gandhi. And Dostoievsky wisely counsels: "Love all God's creation, the whole and every grain of sand in it. Love every leaf, every ray of God's light. Love the animals, love the plants.

Love everything. If you love everything, you will perceive the divine mystery in things. Once you perceive it, you will begin to comprehend it better every day, and you will come at last to love the whole world with an all-embracing love."

SEXUAL LOVE—
MAN TOWARD WOMAN

O. Spurgeon English, M.D.

Sexual Love— Man Toward Woman

O. Spurgeon English, M.D.

None quarrel with statements like "love is unselfish giving" or "love is sharing." On the contrary, such statements are regarded as mere platitudes, so self-evident are their truths. Nor are any distinctions drawn between men and women in this regard. Each is assumed equally to be capable of such giving and such sharing.

Yet, when but a single word is added to these statements, a loud clamor arises. Man's love for woman is accepted as a great, unselfish thing. But man's *sexual* love for woman is regarded by almost everyone as another matter entirely. Few realize that man's longing to give to and share with his mate also exists in his sexual love for her.

The conventional understanding of man's sexual love toward woman is that he pursues her for his purely physical gratification; that he needs her and therefore wants her; that so great is his need that often he will use deceit and aggression to force her to become his sexual partner. The idea that he has love to give and share with her, which is manifested by way of the sexual act, is not at all commonly accepted.

Traditionally it is believed that it is only the woman who has "love" to give in the sexual relationship. Giving love sexually is conceded to be part of her gentle, trusting nature. So ingrained is this concept that, while society believes that woman should only give her love in this fashion after she has been properly courted and married, society "understands" that by reason of her trusting qualities and desire to share her great love, she may sometimes even be induced to indulge in a pre-marital or extra-marital relationship. Society contents itself with the supposed explanation that woman performs the sexual act as a means of expressing her true love, while man performs it because of his physical need and not as an act of love.

Thus, when a man and woman have loved sexually and the man breaks off the relationship, there is generally great sympathy for the woman's unrequited love, while the man is regarded as a brute or a beast or, at best, "just like a man." On the other hand, if the woman breaks off the relationship, she is neither condemned nor vilified; nor is any sympathy extended to the man. Rather, he may be laughed at or ridiculed. He has failed in the role that society has glibly ascribed to him; that of the besieging, pursuing creature whose understanding of love is not on the same plane as woman's, and who, therefore, is of less worth and needs no sympathy.

Is it, then, so surprising that man has little awareness that he has love to give?

That awareness is made even more difficult by society's ready acceptance of shallow observations such as that of Yeats, who alluded to "the desire of the man which is for the woman, and the desire of the woman which is for the desire of the man." Just as man, by reason of his conditioning, seeks, asks, besieges, demands, courts, pleads and, in some instances, takes love from the woman, so woman is by tradition inclined to wait, allow herself to be pursued, wanted, desired, courted, and at times be overcome.

How then can man have very much understanding that he has love to give a woman when actually he is so beset by need and what society calls desire? If he must always play the role of the pursuer and aggressor, how can he be included within the sphere exclusively ascribed to women, that of giving love? For only a few women ever seem to have a comparable aggression in matters of love-making.

Man, it is true, may have many advantages by being permitted to seek, and to demand or ask for love; yet woman's advantages should not be lightly estimated. She has the advantage which comes with passivity. She need never run the risk of being refused, repulsed, or rejected. She exists to be wanted and desired, and can render decision as to whether she will accept man's need for her.

The old saying, "Hell hath no fury like a woman scorned," testifies to the great pain and consequent rage that ensues from the possibility that a woman might ask for love and be denied, or that she might expect love and be disappointed.

It would seem, therefore, that if the concept is to grow, that man has sexual love to give woman which is more than a satisfaction of a physical need, then woman must be taught to understand her own role more consciously. She must put man in the position of being able to give her love. For man cannot give love sexually to a woman who feels that she is the victim of man's desire, sex tension, or animal nature. If the woman takes the negative position that she has no need, and it is only out of the great magnanimity of her heart that she gives herself to man and thereby loves him enough to give him gratification, then the poor fellow will never be in a position to give any love. He can only be the recipient of woman's "lady bountiful" attitude.

Constantly being considered the aggressor, the pursuer, or the supplicant, man finds it next to impossible to regard the sex act as a means of conveying his love to woman. He feels defensive about the whole thing. He is merely being tolerated, made to feel inferior and like a demanding child. He longs for recognition of his own importance in fulfilling the needs of his mate. He does not want to feel tolerated. He seeks for a mutual recognition of the need for love on the part of both sexes, an equal participation, an empathy, better understanding and spontaneity. The mutual recognition and expression of the need would put both man and woman in the position of having something to give. Only with such mutuality can each give and each share.

One need not probe deeply into the study of the fundamental needs and urges of woman to realize that a description of her true desire as being merely to have man desire her, is shallow, devious, and even dishonest. Such a concept totally disregards woman's basic physical self and psychological needs. And yet our poets constantly engage in the deception, our wags wallow in it, and most of us unthinkingly accept it.

As a result of conditioning of this type, both sexes have to do a great deal of pretending and spend a great deal of effort disguising their real natures. Man, so as not to appear "weak," must play the role of the blustering, domineering, even deceptive male when in actuality he wants to give and to share rather than force and dominate.

Woman, on the other hand, for fear she may be thought forward and unmaidenly, feels that her role must be that of submission and passivity, that she has fulfilled her function if she has merely succeeded in making her man desire her and then permitting him to achieve release from his animal-like drives. Yet, at the same time, she knows, deep within herself, that she too wants to be an active partner in this rite of love, that she wants to give and share as well as receive and give release to love's urging.

What is needed is an entirely new approach to the entire problem; an approach which is not founded upon traditional concepts which are really misconceptions of the true motivations of both men and women. We must come to terms with our true selves and adjust our social thinking to the truths we have uncovered.

If we are to seek the truth, then we must be bold enough to seek it everywhere. We must seek it in our sexuality as well as in any other human relation. If the concept is to prosper that man as well as woman has sexual love to give, then we must raise human sexual relations to a plane where they are not feared and condemned, but are considered healthy, wholesome, and even holy.

This we have certainly not achieved as yet. The lack of healthy and wholesome attitudes toward sexuality clearly reflects itself even in our language. When we think of the words that are used for the sexual relationship with a woman—words commonly used by man—we find that not only are they inadequate to describe happily the sexual act, but they are either bantering, impolite, obscene phrases which are rude and lack sophistication, or are clinical terms. They are words and phrases which lack any note of mutuality, dignity, or friendliness. They are either humorous and/or secretive words which refer to the act by nonsense language, or connotationless, dry, impersonal expressions generally used in law, medicine, or science. Most of the phrases connote violence, degradation, ridicule, derision, or invite uncomplimentary comparisons with childlike or animal play.

It is obvious that the semantic reason for the lack of a universally satisfying term or word is that the act is not universally satisfying—that it is not, to strip the matter to its essential, the same to all men. There is no happy, joyful word because the act itself is not always happy and joyful to enough people. Analyze all the usual descriptive phrases and the dissatisfactions with sexual love will appear. Take, for instance, the attitude of a man who associates the act with a word which stems from obscenity and crudity. The act to him, then, may begin in violence and end in derision. In other words, many of the terms are really only mirrors of man's conception of the act itself.

As yet, there is no universal word which can be applied to the act of love-making which expresses the pleasure, happiness, joy, dignity, excitement, adventure, and mutual fulfillment of both sexes. Why is this so? Why are the dissatisfactions so universal?

The answer may lie in the fact that the domestication of the human race has taken a long, long time. The taming of the fundamental, basic instincts took eons of time in the history of man. He has come far from the day when there was the sexual instinct alone. Then, when there was hunger for sex, it was almost immediately satisfied. Now the drive has been recognized and refined from its basic biological nature. And this sublimation has forced a distinction between instinct and libido, the latter being the psychic energy derived from the instincts and consequently available for any degree of blending with ethical, esthetic, and spiritual values.

Modern man still fears his instincts. Few men trust them enough to be relaxed and find life truly enjoyable. For example, man fears his instincts to such an extent that he does not even trust the essential goodness of children. Rather, he warns, frightens, threatens, and coerces them into beliefs which he hopes will insure socially acceptable behavior. He is particularly fearful of his instincts where the sexual relationship is concerned.

Nevertheless, there is a gradual respect slowly arising for the findings of psychiatry and the application of Freudian psychoanalytical theories to everyday living. If this respect is strengthened, and men become less afraid of their primitive impulses, they will find themselves better able to trust the possibility that goodness and beauty are inherent within the physical expression of love-making between men and women.

Heretofore, only the gentle, tender, and intellectual aspects of love have been considered safe, while the more sensuous aspects of love have been considered dangerous and taboo. It will be a constructive step toward resolving our conflicts when society begins to accept man's capabilities of expressing love sexually to the woman. Until society accepts the fact that man has this capacity, he will continue to be a feared and somewhat hated, albeit necessary, object of woman's interest.

All too many women think somewhat as follows: "Man would be all right if he would only be kind to us, take care of us and live peaceably with us without those unesthetic, unpleasant, and demanding appetites for sexual gratifications." So long as women feel that man is not a lover in the true sense of the word, but a predatory nuisance as far as his sexual energy goes, then neither sex will find the potential happiness that awaits mutual expression and enjoyment.

Again, so long as we continue to fear our instincts and so often regard the male child as a little beast, growing up intent on seducing for his personal gratification as many women as he can find, our young men are not likely to regard themselves very highly. Nor are they likely to see themselves as human beings with reservoirs of love, waiting to express that love to their mates with their bodies in marriage.

No new rules are needed. We need only the courage to recognize and give voice socially to the truths we have found. If our cultural mores have made us blind to the truth that sexual love of man toward woman can be joyful and wholesome, we must modify our mores and accept and proclaim that truth. We must no longer instill in our young the conviction that sex is something dirty which man must have and woman must tolerate, albeit sadly. We must not be afraid to acknowledge that sexual love can be an experience of beauty as well as a release of pent-up physical desire.

So long as society keeps nurturing in the growing and developing female a state of anxious apprehension regarding the potential violence and selfishly centered seductive leanings of the male, her own capacity to love comfortably must be correspondingly stunted. How can she ever come to welcome truly the attentions of the male as stimulating, protective, creative, and pleasure-giving, replete with gentleness as well as passion? All too often her reaction is to be on guard against, if not to take flight from the male, particularly if he shows the slightest amorous intentions or, in some cases, even if he only displays a wholesome friendly interest. The more the male is held in distrust, suspicion, and even contempt, the more he is prone to grab, snatch, deceive, and even coerce the female who fears and despises him. If only bad things are expected of people, they are not likely to produce much that is good. Consequently, man suffers from a society that does not consider him a good and loving creature, capable of giving great pleasure and creating great beauty.

Society must begin now to accept the criterion of beauty and pleasure as a purpose of the act of love instead of regarding it solely as a utilitarian function to enable reproduction. Man and woman must recognize that what is biologically and psychologically utilitarian need not be stark, ugly, a thing to be hidden, an act to be despised. On the contrary, they must realize that an object or emotion to be utilitarian must produce the utmost function, and that in the case of the sex act, beauty and pleasure are that utmost function.

In fine, man must learn that he is now sufficiently well organized to ease his concern over protection of the weak, and admit pleasure as the concern of the sex act. Many already disregard society's "utilitarian" consideration of sex and admit its pleasures. Man must give dignity to sexual pleasure. In some instances, it is the pleasure which can give strength and thus protection to the weak, since happiness is one of the health-giving emotional states.

This creation of beauty is what mankind, in other spheres, regards as the greatest object of life. What greater creation of beauty than to produce for and with a human you feel in sympathy with, in empathy with, the joy of love? Reproduction is, of course, the original societal consideration, but man should have learned by this time that there is danger in having one viewpoint and not adding to happiness with new knowledge.

To produce and raise a human being to the plane of happiness and productivity is or should be the zenith of selflessness. No human can be happy or productive without pleasure and beauty. The creation, the conceiving, of a child is no less part of the production of a happy person than protecting him once he is born.

Society is inconsistent in saying that the act of love should be solely utilitarian and only indirectly pleasurable. The pleasure of offspring is an extension of the sexual instinct. The pleasure of loving is another extension. Both are outlets, releases for that impetus to create and produce, sustain and live, love and enjoy.

It has been difficult for society to accept any such formulation because it seems to indicate that if there is not fear and hate, sexual expression will become "free." However, there is great confusion of thinking in regard to the concept of free love. Love should be free, yes—free of shame, disgust, fear, hostility. Love should be freely blended with beauty, courtesy, consideration, and the golden rule. To make love free does not mean to create more promiscuity, more fornication, or more adultery. In point of fact it would almost surely lead to less, since consideration, kindness, and the golden rule, applied to sexual relations, would bring them into line with long-existing moral laws.

How can we achieve the objective of getting society to

accept and openly acknowledge the potential beauty of man's sexual love toward woman? The answer is, as always, through education. But there are many forces which oppose such education.

The Christian religion grudgingly admits that in the consummation of marriage, man worships the woman physically, that he expresses his love physically as well as spiritually. However, this is not yet considered a safe subject to be taught in the church. Indeed, many religious leaders are opposed to any philosophy of sexual love being taught in the school. They keep insisting, with obvious inconsistency, that it be taught at home by parents, who, of course, are a product of these same schools and churches which have found the philosophy of sex too wicked, too dangerous, too personal, or too "disturbing" to be discussed openly. This from our schools and churches which are the institutions which are looked upon as the repositories of the utmost "good" in our society! They are the ones who should be working toward a blending of their goodness with the supposed wickedness of sexuality.

If in this contribution we have merely succeeded in pointing up the negative light in which man's sexual love is being held, we may at least have helped to start a trend toward constructive thinking about the problem. We believe that man, whether he be a religious leader, parent, educator, or husband, must examine the basis of his fears and prejudices about sexuality. Is he afraid of wholesale fornication and adultery? Has he any proof that knowledge of sex and education as to its most creative potentialities will produce a greater prevalence of these things? Has he ever stopped to think that good ideas in relation to the sexual drives can come about only by admitting and discussing the nature of sexuality, so that socially constructive concepts can be woven into the personality fabric? We might even ask whether man is prejudiced against (or, perhaps, even jealous about) permitting the younger generation to have a less conflicted, easier, and happier orientation toward the sexual problem than he himself has had.

Despite these obstacles, we must nevertheless strive to raise the level of man's understanding of his sexual love for woman. We should try to get woman to give up her fear that the male is only a predatory, sex-hungry, inconsiderate, violent creature. We should stop trying to put a wedge between the sexes by teaching fear and mutual hostility. We should try to define the whole nature of love, including its sexual aspect. The loving man is neither a Don Juan nor a rapist. The loving woman has no less control of her sexual activity than the frightened, frigid, hateful one. Each could be taught higher and more useful, more beautiful, more satisfactory love relations.

But such education can never be effective until we can discard fear and prudery. We still have love and fear sadly mixed up. Parents say, "I love my child so I do not want him to learn anything about sexual love until he is married. Because of my love for him, I want to protect him from the evils of sexuality." These parents must learn that love is a total emotional reaction. In order to serve its end, it must include instruction and guidance in every facet of human activity, including sexuality, in its proper time and place. To integrate sexuality into the loving personality, it must be taught as naturally as all the other facts, attitudes, and values of life are taught.

When this day arrives, as yet it can, if we become skillful enough in the communication of ideas, then someone will undoubtedly come along with the word which will express "sexual love—man toward woman." It will combine the vitality, the vigor, the warmth, the affection, the adventure, the variety, the thrill, the satisfaction, the condensation of so much experience and happy memories in an act which can repeatedly bring fulfillment and renewal of inspiration to both sexes.

SEXUAL LOVE—
WOMAN TOWARD MAN

Marynia F. Farnham, M.D.

Sexual Love— Woman Toward Man

Marynia F. Farnham, M.D.

In the concept of love, we are fond of thinking, man has a unique quality and a peculiar distinction, one which dignifies his life and invests it with a benign power which gives a special quality to his living, provides him with a motivation beyond the immediacy of the physical, and is capable of restraining his aggressiveness and directing his energies toward peaceable and lofty ends. Women have often been thought of as particularly capable of and susceptible to love. Their love for men has always been a preoccupation of the poets and dreamers. It, like the love of men for women, retains a capacity to excite and charm, to fascinate and enchant. This love theme is presented and analyzed in ways ranging from the most brutally mechanical to those most remotely romantic.

Throughout the history of civilization it has been variously considered. The Greeks seem to have had no very great opinion of it—nor of women, for that matter. The sexual relation between men and women was accepted as a necessity, but one which could well be postponed until youthful romanticism had been drained off during adolescence. In this way, there was less likelihood of having men's minds deflated from the truly profound considerations of politics and philosophy. It was regarded with dignity, to be sure, but not to be confused with the essentially great considerations of life to which every adult man was expected to give his best thought and effort. The Roman world brought to it a composed and noble attitude which would not have satisfied any modern woman. The man was considered the final arbiter of the situation, and his decisions did not necessarily take account of the woman's wishes. He had the freedom and she had the role of dependent subordinate in everything.

Not until the Christian era, however, did the idea of romantic love, as we know it, put in its appearance. It is this notion which is today in our mind when the word "love" is used. The earlier civilizations separated sex and love, regarding the former with much less intensity as an accepted and necessary part of life. The latter was the noble, mutual devotion of any two individuals as expressed when Antony says in *Julius Caesar:* "I am no orator . . . but . . . a plain blunt man, that loves my friend." At its inception, the Christian world was little disposed to admire the love of men and women in the sexual sense, and the Pauline philosophy said so. It was thought better to direct the animal impulses of men and to ensure the continuance of the race by controlled methods rather than have things get out of hand. "Better to marry than to burn."

In the world of the Middle Ages, the modern sentiment of romantic love emerges. This brought out the idealization of the feminine, placing her beyond the reach of men's coarser natures. The highest expression of these strivings is to be found in the great love myths of the Western World: Tristan and Iseult, Heloïse and Abelard. Here the fatal outcome is always the same: renunciation and death. This has held sway over men's minds until the present day. The notion of the chaste and beautiful woman, untarnished by the carnal and bestial, is one of the dominating ideas of the Western mind. By the time the modern era dawned, the Victorians continued the romantic ideal of male-female love, accompanying it with an attempt to disencumber it altogether from sex, which continued to be regarded as a disastrous tarnishing of a refined and spiritual emotion.

All these past ideas had something in common in their attitudes toward the relations between the sexes. The cornerstone of the whole outlook was the assumption that the man was the dominant partner and the controlling spirit in the relationship. As a corollary of this, the assumption was that only the male was cursed (or blessed, as it was later interpreted) by the possession of feelings of lust or physical desire and passion. The female was endowed with a fantasy character entirely purified of the carnal. We say "fantasy" because it is easy to see that this was exactly what it was. The fact of physical passion was not new or unknown. Nothing we can find out about our early predecessors would lead us to believe that physical sexual feeling is a late emergence. It has always been with us. But somewhere along the line it came to be regarded as a disaster and a guilt-arousing possession which should be denied and controlled, not simply taken for granted and accepted without any particular attitude, somewhat as the need for food is taken for granted. This dubious addition to the sexual attitudes of Western man seems to arise from the Judeo-Christian teachings and thinking, and we have been coping with it ever since. There was introduced the idea of guilt. This is inherent in the myths of Judaic history and is clear in the symbolism of the Genesis story, with its transparent recitation of the dangers, punishments, and guilts attendant upon growing up and entering into the sexual aspects of life. What are the apple and the serpent but old symbols for the female and male elements? And what is the tree of the knowledge of good and evil except the symbol of the throwing off of childhood innocence in the sense of a "not knowing" consciously and living in fantasy as every child does?

The modern world has tried to say good-bye to all this. With its inception, man was catapulted into the position of having to deal rationally with a part of his nature which had always been felt as apart from the rational and was viewed as inherently a moral and extra-rational problem. This began with the new scientific period of which we are now a part. Everything could be known, explained, and understood, and so could, of course, all of man's nature— his strivings and needs. Among these needs the sexual was conspicuous. Sigmund Freud was the first exponent of this kind of thinking. He brought into consciousness, one might say, much that had not before been allowed to be there, and put forth the notion that this too could be known and understood, governed by reason and accepted, as all things can be which are susceptible to reasonable analysis. There was then ushered in the sexual revolution, of which we are the inheritors and the consequences of which we are the uneasy possessors.

The modern interpretations after Freud go rather simply. Possibly, deceptively so. The sexual impulse is a universal one, being the possession of children as well as of adults. This last is one of Freud's really revolutionary ideas. The proper expression of the impulse is vital to our mental health, and its repression, or the failure to find expression for it, is fraught with dangers and even disasters to our best development. Fundamentally, such inhibition leads to neurosis and neurosis means faulty functioning and is to be avoided at all costs. As usual with prophets, their interpreters have played fast and loose with the words of the prophet. Freud's dicta were widely distorted and misrepresented until we arrived at some notions that any attempt to curb the sexual impulse was sure to lead to trouble and the best and healthiest thing to do was to express the impulse in any way and at any time and under any circumstances which seemed pleasing. These were counsels of anarchy and far from those of Freud, if he could be said to have done any counseling at all. Out of an attempt to put these supposed counsels to work, we have had the eras of wild experimentation and anarchic so-called "liberation." Rebellion against controls of any sort was the cardinal virtue of that not-too-distant period, and sex was to be regarded as all other "instincts" or "appetites," to be indulged in with casualness and without self-consciousness. This was presumed to usher in a period of mental vigor and lack of inhibition which would permit man to enter once more into the Garden of Eden.

Not everything was realized from these doctrines that their promoters had hoped for, and those who were beguiled by the ideas of freedom were often disappointed and felt that they had been betrayed by an overzealous campaign of persuasion. Satisfaction did not follow from indulgence, and often these two seemed to have no relation to each other. The golden future seemed as far off as ever and there was some disposition to carp about these misrepresentations. Little else could have been expected, as this has usually been the result of the enthusiastic embrace of a new and exciting theory. There is always the necessary period of re-evaluation. It is that period in which we find ourselves today and which we want to examine as it relates to what we can now tell about the requirements for good and satisfying love relations between a man and a woman. Some of the dust has settled, and we can see a little further into ourselves and sort out some of the excessive and unrealistic expectations. We know a little more about what the human psyche is capable of and what it is not, and we can speak with a little more authority about what the essential elements of human love are. We are less afraid today to speak about love and to acknowledge that there is still much that is unknowable than we were when we had just emerged from a period of entirely unknowing mystery.

Love is an emotion which arises in the earliest period of life and goes out toward the person who provides the satisfactions which are indispensable to the survival and well-being of the young individual. Love is the answer to the security provision. What provides security is loved. One may say that love, in its early expression, is an economic device to induce the gratifier to continue to give the indispensable care and attention. The young child has nothing else to give to the mother who gives generously and open-heartedly of her attention and tender care and allays the infant's feelings of anxiety for his own welfare. But love he can and does give in full measure and without stint. In exchange for this love, his mother is willing to give on her part without stint all that the baby wants and needs, and all that will make him feel safe and secure, and so without fear or anxiety. This is the same at the beginning for both boy and girl babies; this is the foundation and rudiment of love. As growth proceeds, there is a steady difference and widening departure between the two sexes. They must and do learn to some degree through all their experiences to interpret love, that is, the way of getting gratification through giving it, through the intermediation of all the elements of their constitutions, their biological experiences, personal and cultural, and their physical and psychological organization.

In spite of the fact that contemporary society tends in the direction of lessening the emphasis on the differences between the sexes and attaching more importance to their similarities than to their divergences, there is no way of eradicating those differences, and they still play a determining role in molding the adult man and woman. Consider the girl child in all her aspects and in all the ways in which she is reared and influenced throughout her development. To begin with, she starts with the physical attributes of femininity, in the form of her procreative organization, with ovaries and uterus as the core of it. This imbues her with an inescapable mandate to be the receptor and carrier in her reproductive role. It sets the requirement for her to be ultimately the passive and patient actor in the sexual drama. Her body demands it and is functionally set for it. She is structurally an individual made to be penetrated and not, as with her opposite, the male, to penetrate. Her entire nature must pay some tribute to this fact and its inevitability.

It is no longer at all reasonable to think of the human being as an envelope in which are inserted two entirely distinct parts, the mind and the body. We know altogether too much about the influence of these elements one on the other and their infinite intermingling and interdependence to be content with the "divided being" idea. The animal is all of a piece, with all its various systems acting and interacting together and upon each other. It is stretching things to the point of the unbearable to imagine that the physical organization of the female, distinct as it is from that of the male, has not a kind of matching or sympathetic psychic organization. The many ways in which special kinds of characteristics are linked with one sex or the other in the genetic or hereditary scheme are evidence of this matching. So inevitably we have a human organization which is called female and its characters are as we have sketched them: a tendency to passivity and endurance; to be a receiver of power and a nurturer of it; to tend toward dependency and a need for a supportive relationship; to look for the long-lasting and reliable; to approach living and to solve problems with a high admixture of intuition or unconscious thinking, as it might be called; to have a capacity and even a predilection for a tender and protective attitude toward the helpless and needful young; to prefer a subjective rather than an objective approach to life.

These we may call the natural tendencies which can be encouraged and cultivated or suppressed and opposed by the society and culture in which the individual is reared. All education and training in the social climate of today is toward playing them down rather than encouraging them. Boys and girls are reared much alike, with the same privileges and expectations to a large degree. This is not only a formal matter of being taught the same curricula in the classrooms. It is more subtly the manner of their acceptance in the home and in the society whose influence the home communicates to them. Today, the girl is expected to play a dual role and perform in much the same way as the boy, while still continuing her functions as wife and mother. These demands have tended to force her to suppress some of her basically feminine characteristics. But they cannot bring about the eradication of the fundamentally feminine. These can only be driven underground and their expression made more difficult or even distorted.

In harmony with these tendencies, which are dependent upon larger forces arising from many sources not connected basically with the nature of men and women but with extraneous matters, there has been a comprehensive movement to induce women to give up and not act upon some of their basic needs. Thus they have found themselves in a position where they have been influenced to surrender one of their most profound needs, that of long-lasting and durable relations with the male on behalf of the care of the young, in exchange for what has seemed like freedom of choice of action and of partner in that action—equally with the male. Likewise, they have tended to allow themselves to be urged away from their function of nurturing and caring for their children because of this same argument—that their equality with the man requires them to do much more than that simple (or supposedly simple) task. In all of these exertions, they have often been faced with the fact that with the loss of their passivity and receptivity, much of the savor has gone out of their relationship with the male, and it has disappointed their expectations, leaving them half satisfied and men even less so, as their masculinity has been thereby reduced in their own estimation.

One can trace in careful detail the play and interplay of these various forces on the traditional and constitutional temperament of women. It has been greatly influenced by over-all cultural trends, as the shape of a tree is by the prevailing winds. In answer to all these calls and expectations, today's woman has responded with a vigorous effort to adjust herself. By yielding here and going underground there, distorting in this area and inhibiting in another, she has somehow been able to fulfill these various and multifarious requirements. She has managed to maintain something of a uniqueness and specificity of temperament so that there is still the feminine mind which contrasts with the masculine, and the truly feminine mood and spirit remain.

The love relation flourishes and develops to the finest degree only when there is confidence and security between the partners. For women, this must mean a durability in the relationship, a lastingness which can provide the inner protection which is as much needed as the outer material protection. In spite of the fact that today a woman need not fear material destitution if she be left alone with children to rear, she will fear as much the inner desolation and the excess demand on her strength as she would fear the other. At its core, the love relation for women must contain the capacity for complete surrender to and with the partner in that relation. Particularly, and in harmony with her psycho-biological organization, a woman cannot experience total gratification unless she does achieve this total yielding of herself. Her entire background and her physical being play into this. From her structure, she is the receptor of the male organ in the sexual embrace. She must be able to regard it as the source of gratification, and wholly without danger to her, if she is to be able to give her own body to gratifying powers of the male body. If her attitude toward the male is tarnished with feelings of fear or envy, rivalry or contempt, it is all too obvious that she cannot bring to her relationship the compliance and loving receptivity indispensable to gratification and real love. At the very base of it all must lie her longing for total fulfillment and ultimate function in her wish to be pregnant and to bear children, to nurture them and return to the man in their mutual child the visible evidence of their unyielding love and devotion.

There is a deeply felt answer here to a profound metaphysical truth. As the man, freely and without withholding of any sort, gives his germinal substance to the loved woman, she receives it and holds and nourishes it for a long patient time, during which his function is in abeyance and unneeded. She then has the unique experience of perfection. She contains for that seeming long but still brief time herself, the essence of the male love object (the penis) and the child. If her relation is one of love, she will wish to give to the man this child to share and still be willing to nurture and care for it in the special way open to her alone but without wishing to make this the basis for taking the child as her own possession. So, in her wish for love, she brings both the capacity to receive and accept, to endure and wait, but the capacity too for sharing and returning, for giving greatly to the child and to the man. At her best, that giving is untainted by possessiveness or narrow egotism. In these desirable circumstances, both partners have an opportunity to express themselves openly and fully and to find completeness in each other through their mutual regard and devotion.

This aspect of the love relation has been timeless and it is not less true now than it ever was. But some things have been added in a certain way to make the relationship more even and more expansive for both, as well as to eradicate certain discrepancies which had grown up in the woman's part of the operation. When the home began to be displaced by the encroachments of industry, it is now well known that women suffered deeply from the disenfranchisement which followed. They insensibly became more and more removed from real life and less and less important in any real sense of the word—beyond their childbearing abilities. The rebellion against this brought the rivalry and enmity between men and women which has become so conspicuous a part of modern life. Women were the "outs" and they wanted to be the "ins." Due consideration had to be given to these needs because it is obvious that no society is going to make the best use of women if it neglects their intellectual and artistic capacities and allows no outlet for them except at the price of giving up their valuable and irreplaceable femininity and its derivatives.

But that does not need to be. For in today's love relationship, if the needs of both partners are to be met and the potentialities of both are to be allowed to prosper, the woman must also be the full intellectual partner of the man. The day is past when she can answer the demands of her own nature or satisfy the needs of her partner if she elects to limit herself to the expression of the physical-emotional sides of her nature only. This is actually not new. Men and women had a full partnership in every sense of the word until their separation was brought about by the unexpected and disturbing effects of the Industrial Revolution. Then they were under no necessity to be separated and so sharply divided as they worked each at his own part of the common task in or near the home. The present deterioration of the relationship came about through the misfortunes necessarily accompanying a time of revolutionary readjustment. It is this partnership, today often missing, which is the indispensable element in a truly great love relationship.

In this way, balance and fullness are achieved. In such a relationship the woman is able fully to express her womanly nature through a completely secure and total surrender to a partner with whom she is in harmony, to whom she expects to give her entire nature, and from whom she can confidently expect loyal and lasting devotion as well as sexual gratification. When there is added to this an intellectual compatibility and participation, there can be a love relation which permits room for the expression of a satisfying femininity without the sacrifice of any of the woman's capacities and an opportunity for her to make the most complete use of her total personality.

Love of Friends

Alvin Johnson

Love of Friends

Alvin Johnson

Love of friends: how can one write of an emotion that flows to the utmost confines of human life, and beyond life itself? For do I not often evoke, waking and in dreams, the living image of friends who have gone before? They are still my friends. And so are Plato and Horace and Pliny the Younger, with whom I have had many hours of sweet converse across the narrow strait of the fleeting centuries.

And can one limit the category of friends to the human species alone? How about my childhood friend, Antonia, a pretty little Indian pony colt, who the day after she was born fixed her bright eyes on me and set me down as a human colt, her fellow and playmate. How often I'd slip through the wires of the pasture fence, to have the thrill of this little creature galloping up to me, as if to run me down, then braking with all four little hooves, to step forward and press her velvety nuzzle against my cheek. I loved Tony, passionately, and Tony loved me.

Love of friends: it is a hard subject for an extrovert, whose natural disposition is to be absorbed in what he sees and hears, not in the hearing and seeing and the wonderful creature who hears and sees. It is a bad subject for a man whose discipline of life has selected for study wide uniformities, chains of cause and effect, where the effect bears a measurable relation to the cause. There are no uniformities in the love of friends. And the effect seldom bears closer relation to the cause than my majestic old oak tree to the selfish squirrel who dug a superfluous acorn into the ground, for a future breakfast, in the days when George Washington was still a surveyor. The squirrel forgot the acorn: hence the noble tree waving its old arms over the shining river. Explanation enough in terms of cause and effect? Perhaps.

If I am to write of love of friends I must write naively. What I have to say must be read naively. Lilienthal's colored friend asserted that what he had to say was so simple it took the mind of a child to understand it. Lend me the child mind that is in the heart of every mind that really lives.

The ways and modes of love of friends are innumerable. There is the love at first sight, and the love that imperceptibly develops out of long association. There is the love that lasts a day and the love that shines serenely through a lifetime. There is the love that is pure devotion and the love alloyed with the quid-pro-quo principle. There is love that binds just two persons together against all the world and the love that flourishes in confraternities and gangs. I could extend the catalogue, but what is the use? I'd never get to the end of it.

There are authorities who would confine the conception of love of friends to the love that permanently binds two friends together. So Cicero, describing the love of Scipio Africanus and Laelius, declared that literature offered scarcely two or three instances of such love. He had in mind Damon and Pythias, Orestes and Pylades, perhaps Achilles and Patroclus. The modern commentator usually insinuates David and Jonathan in the Notes.

Is this close, enduring love between a pair of friends actually so rare? I'd venture to guess that Cicero might have found many instances in the Roman legions of his day, among men held together by their terms of service for more than half a lifetime, men who campaigned together on the plateaus of Spain, the jagged hills of Dalmatia, the fever-stricken coasts of North Africa, among the wily cut-throats of Asia Minor. There must have been men who shared toil and wounds and disease together, hopes and despairs, who found themselves indissolubly bound together. And when their thirty-five years of service were over, the wise Roman statesmen planted them on little farms, side by side, that their friendship might continue until death.

I have encountered a dozen or more such pairs of friends in frontier settlements. And I conclude that this type of friendship is rare only in the experience of the intellectuals. Permanent devotion does not go well with intellectual ambition.

But I pause to pay my respects to an explanation of "dyadic" friendships advanced by writers in the decadent period of Rome and restored to currency by one of the great geniuses of our time, Sigmund Freud—homosexualism. The explanation looks more cogent when it is applied to esthetes than when it is applied to rugged Roman soldiers, dragging their female captives from camp to camp, or to robust pioneers in the mountain country, each with his "woman" caring for his cabin.

Since I am writing to the child in the reader's mind, I may be permitted to tell a little story of my childhood. A new family had moved into the neighborhood. They came in a prairie schooner, from all over the West. They had a boy Johnny, seven, and I was six. I loved Johnny at first sight. He was beautiful, with curly dark hair. My hair was tow. His brown eyes were like a diamond bright, but my blue eyes were dull as lead.

Of course I loved Johnny.

Besides, he was a hero. He had galloped over the sagebrush desert beside his father with a pack of Piute Indians pursuing with scalping knives. His father's horse and his pony were faster than the Indian mounts and Johnny had turned again and again to shout insults to the grimly disappointed braves. My love for Johnny mounted cloud-high on the wings of admiration.

Our families visited together a family stocked with big, coarse sons. They took Johnny and me to the barn, and decided that we should run a horse race on the road before the barn. They saddled two enormous man-eating horses, put us in the saddles in spite of wailing protests, and gave the horses good cuts with a blacksnake. The horses reared and galloped down the road, I hanging to the saddle pommel for dear life. But Johnny clung to the pommel and his horse's mane, shrieking to heaven. When the horses got tired and jogged back to the barn the big boys took us off and gave me an apple as winner in the race. Johnny was blubbering hysterically and ran to the house for comfort in his mother's arms.

My love for Johnny poured out of my heart like milk from a kicked-over bucket. Johnny a hero? No, just a blowhard, as we expressed it.

When I told this story to Dr. Fritz Wittels, psychoanalyst, he said: "The case is simple. Childish homosexualism." One hesitates to quarrel with a psychoanalyst, yet there is a circumstance that made me doubt the explanation. Two years earlier, when my sister brought me to visit the school, a big girl, Hattie, took me by the hand and led me around the schoolyard. The touch of Hattie's soft hand, the sweet cadences of her voice, the glowing splendor of her dark eyes composed a mystery that remained with me for years, until I could understand it. Hattie had made me heterosexual for life. I loved Hattie, but my love was something quite different from my love for Johnny. Nothing could have disillusioned me of Hattie. Alas, I never saw her again.

What is it that draws human beings, and indeed others of the higher vertebrates, together as friends and holds them together for shorter or longer periods of time? One force is the need of mutual aid. I do not scorn this motive of interest in friendships any more than I scorn the forces that bring the high-born lady to the arms of the rich bourgeois. We were cast out upon this earth, to manage as best we can.

But I do not regard the motive of advantage as the dominant force that draws all the world together in friendship associations. The essential need lies deeper.

One cannot live to himself alone for any length of time. Consider the lot of a castaway on a desert island.

> "I am out of humanity's reach.
> I must finish my journey alone,
> Never hear the sweet music of speech;
> I start at the sound of my own."

The poet, living in a medium of words, naturally gave first place to the sweet music of speech. But the need of social intercourse can be met satisfactorily among deaf mutes. Glances, gestures, can be made to suffice. A man does not go mad in solitude if he is on friendly terms with his horse. Or even with sheep.

Some years ago I met a great sheep man, a Basque named Echegary. He was inveighing against the stupidity of the Government, which would not let him bring over more Basque shepherds—sheepherders, in Western parlance. He had winter feed enough, and there was grass enough on the mountain side for twenty sheep units of 800 head. He was limited to seven units, by his inability to get Basques.

"Must you have Basques?" I asked, "Can't you use Yankees, Germans, Scandinavians?"

"No; they all go crazy. They don't love sheep. Suppose a sheep is pushed over a cliff and breaks a leg. A Yankee sheepherder knocks it in the head. A Basque carries it to his wagon, puts the leg in splints, plucks grass for the sheep and feeds it his own food. A sheep isn't worth that, but the Basque has to do it. He loves his sheep."

You set out in the spring from the winter folds and lead eight hundred sheep, half little lambs, toward the high mountain pastures. You have six months' food and drink in your wagon, and for six months you will never meet a human being. The Yankee sheepherder, returned to winter quarters, is "queer." Very queer. The Basque is normal, for he loves his sheep. He has herded sheep on the mountains for three thousand years. They are in his soul.

Life is made up of experiences, mostly widely spaced, mostly incapable of making by themselves a sharp impression on the mind. If you have someone with whom you communicate, an experience becomes two experiences, the event and the telling, and the telling magnifies the event. You shoot a coyote. Well, what of it? But you tell your friend about it, and all the maneuvers you made to get in range of the coyote, the eagerness with which you aimed and pulled the trigger, the spasmodic death struggle of the "varmint," assume intensified reality. Your experience lives, and you live, by the magic of friendship.

You are working late in a field, to finish a strip of plowing for the morrow's sowing. The dusk is gathering, the cold evening spring wind refrigerates your sweaty shirt; your heels are chafed, you are dog-tired and hungry. Your horses turn their faces pathetically upon you. They are tired too, hungry, chafed by collar and harness, their sensitive sides shivering under the wind. "Couldn't we call it a day?" they seem to say. The misery of your experience somehow lightens, with the sense of unity with your four-footed friends.

"Misery loves company." That is the truth.

I have given what I consider the fundamental function of love of friends, the vivification of experience through communication. But there is an associated function, the enrichment of life through addition of your friend's experience to your own. I can't go tarpon fishing with my friend Leo. But when he comes back with an account of how he hooked the tarpon, how he played him to weariness of man and fish, how he finally got the flopping monster on board —why, I've experienced tarpon by proxy!

But I must hasten on to the most important function in love of friends, leadership and followership.

Rarely are two friends evenly matched. The one leads, the other follows. Neither could thrive without the other. You think of something that ought to be done. Will your friend go along with you? Then your idea is insofar validated. Or you just can't think of anything to do. Your strand of experience is running thin. Your energetic friend descends upon you with an eager project. You take fire, and your experience spins rich life.

The ways of leadership and followership are so various that they deserve a whole treatise. They are beset with mixed motives. Do I follow a friend because he stirs me, or because I expect to get something out of it? Suppose we consider a specific case, Pompey and Caesar on the eve of Pharsalia.

Pompey was the idol of the ambitious aristocrats. That evening they were confident of victory. The most ambitious assembled in Pompey's tent to divide up the spoils of the anticipated victory. "I will take a consulship!" "You? Why, I have a far better claim on it." "I'll take the fat province of Asia. My fortunes are at an ebb; I have to repair them." "The gods help Asia if you get it. There will be no blood left in the province." And so they disputed and almost came to sword play.

There was no assembly of greedy ambitions in Caesar's tent. His army meant to win, but knew they would have to pay for it. Pompey had twice as many men, better fed, better rested, better equipped. Caesar, as was his wont, went about bareheaded among his soldiers, with a brave word or two to the commonest legionary he found awake. A centurion with face cicatrized into a raised map of a mountain province accosted him.

"Hail, Caesar! After tomorrow you may never again see my face. But you will say I paid the debt I owe you, Caesar."

The victory was Caesar's. The centurion exhibited prodigies of valor and was slain. But as Caesar used to say, a brave man dies only once. A coward dies repeatedly.

Max Weber and his disciples characterize Caesar's kind of leadership as "charismatic"—a leadership of love-compelling charm. Roman history offers a better example of charismatic leadership in Scipio Africanus.

The fortunes of Rome were at a low ebb. Hannibal was raging at will through Italy, destroying any Roman army that dared to face him. The two Roman armies in Spain, commanded by the father and uncle of Scipio Africanus, had been destroyed, and only a toehold remained to the Romans in the Spanish peninsula, whose resources were vital to Hannibal's Italian campaign. Young Scipio—he was twenty-two—rose up to demand the province of Spain. Quintus Fabius Maximus and the Old Guard were outraged; a brash boy, identified with the subversive liberal crowd, daring to undertake the most crucial and most difficult military enterprise of the time.

But young Scipio knew how to avail himself of the force of "charism." From adolescence he had taken care to present his splendid figure wherever Romans assembled. He made their love his private possession. And in spite of the opposition of the Old Guard he won the command in Spain, and by his energy and luck, but more by his charismatic power over high and low, he expelled the Carthaginians from Spain. Against the violent opposition of Fabius and the Old Guard he crossed into Africa, forcing Carthage to recall Hannibal, whom Scipio crushed, ending the Carthaginian war.

There is not one recorded detail in the military life of Scipio which does not exhibit him as a man of unexampled humanity, generosity, courage, and charm. Neutrals, and even enemies, had only to meet him to be captivated and won over. I have no doubt that it was from Scipio that his protégé Terence drew the famous sentiment, *"Homo sum. I am a man. There is nothing human I consider alien to me."*

Cicero devotes his essay *De Amicitia* to the love of Scipio and Laelius. All through his campaigns Scipio had kept Laelius at his side. If there was a difficult but highly honorable expedition to be undertaken, on land or sea, Scipio put it under the command of Laelius. The two friends retired together from army and politics and joined in the enterprise of enriching Roman culture by acclimatizing Greek art, literature, philosophy, ethics of life, and law. It was a vast and fascinating undertaking, occupying the two friends to the end of their lives. How could they have failed to be inseparable?

I may be permitted one more classical example from the charismatic Socratic Circle. With the strong hand of Pericles relaxed by death, Athens had become a mobocracy, with generals competing for the doubtful honor of pushing the ruinous Peloponnesian War, with conspiracies forming all over, with sedition and downright treason rife. The young Alcibiades, a man with abundant charism of his own, was ardent for action but his mind was so tangled by conflicting ideas and plans that he could not see where he could head in. He knew that the one group in Athens that seemed to know what it wanted was the Socratic Circle. He resolved to try it.

He came a skeptic, to see what that unattractive old fellow Socrates was doing. He listened a while to conversation which at first seemed desultory but which, in its progress, developed into certainty. The splendor of Socrates' mind loomed above his dull body. Alcibiades was fired with enthusiasm. The charism of Socrates had enslaved him. Coming as he did from circles that identified love with sex he made up his mind to offer himself to Socrates. But the old philosopher gently diverted him from mundane thoughts to the high serene world of ideas. Alcibiades left Socrates a changed man. He knew now what he wanted to do, what he had to do. He would win the wealth and power of Sicily and return to make himself an aristocratic and more philosophic Pericles.

The Old Guard defeated him and Athens plunged ahead toward her ruin. Perhaps Alcibiades, Socratized, could have saved her.

Charismatic leadership has played an important part in our American history. The power of Washington lay less in his command of statecraft than in his power to inspire the love of his lieutenants and of the people. So too of Lincoln, Theodore Roosevelt; and one of the outstanding examples of charism was Franklin D. Roosevelt. In the early days of his administration the men composing his Brain Trust were lifted with a fanatical zeal to serve him. And if the charism lost its hold on some, it won new converts to Roosevelt's ideas and policies.

It will be said that there is something lacking in the relation between the charismatic leader and his followers. Love demands mutuality. The plain citizen may have loved Napoleon or Franklin D. Roosevelt, but those leaders had never even heard of the plain citizen. The existence of a leader, however, draws his followers together in groups, creating friendly relations among them. Also, every leader has his enemies who are drawn together as friends by their common hatred.

Love of friends is essential to a healthy spiritual and mental life. It is best when love can be mutual, but it is good to love even where there is no return. It is at its highest when two persons are bound together indissolubly in love, but for most persons love is directed toward several friends; and is transient, moving from one object of love or many to new objects. Go to the twenty-fifth anniversary of your college class. You will meet men you loved, in the bright days on the campus. You love them still; yes, but your common experience of that time has turned today into reminiscence, sweet, but without nutriment for the soul. No man leaves a class reunion without a vague feeling of sadness. My classmate Billy, whom I loved, is now successful, stout, and jolly. There is no thrill in him for me. My classmate Harry, next in my love, is thin, somewhat bent and worried. Poor Harry; he deserved better of the world. But I can't make amends in behalf of the world.

This transitory character of love of friends is a modern phenomenon, particularly American. We are all on the make and move from one environment with its complex of experience to another scheme of life. We make new friends to share our new experiences; we can keep up the old ones only reminiscently. Our modern family system, with its forced exclusiveness, has also its effects upon love of friends. How many farewell parties we all attend for friends about to disappear behind the silken curtain of matrimony!

"Marriage and death and division make barren our lives."

A good wife replaces many friends in the nourishment of the spirit. And a wife who regards her husband's friends as a menace to her empire, who sits up when he is out with them, "nursing her wrath to keep it warm," is an effective agent in the dissolution of friendships.

It was not so in Greece, where men lived for the most part

in unchanging status and where wives, confined to the women's quarters, expected their husbands to go abroad.

Lest I be set down as an enemy of marriage, let me say that I recognize that the best and most creative dyadic association of friends is between husband and wife, with conjugal love grown imperceptibly into love of friends.

> "We clomb the hill thegither;
> And monie a canty day, John,
> Weve had wi' ane anither.
> Nu we maun totter down, John,
> But hand in hand we'll go,
> And sleep thegither at the foot,
> John Anderson, my jo."

Brill the psychoanalyst used to say, "There can be no neuroses where the relation of husband and wife is live and wholesome." I will add: no neuroses where the love of friends flows in a rich, clear stream. But in this world of today there are too many neuroses. We too often let the art of making true friends yield to the arts that seem closer to our private interests and ambitions.

The Love of Mankind

H. M. Kallen

The Love of Mankind

H. M. Kallen

What, when you come down to cases, does anybody love when he loves mankind?

If his beloved object is all the people there are, it adds up to more than two billion men, women, and children in every conceivable phase and form of the personal struggle to live and to grow. Each and every one of them counts to himself as at least One—unique, precious, indefeasible. He lives and labors, eats, drinks, loves, quarrels, and worships with numbers of others close at hand who similarly account themselves Ones, and their reciprocal doings incarnate the manners and morals, the customs and traditions that define them as a community and make up the way of life which they learned from their elders and which their youngsters learn from them.

This way of life, again, sustains an individuality of its own with its own collective singularity, its own modes of striving to preserve and strengthen its selfhood of forms and functions. Each such collective singularity is a culture, and mankind counts thousands upon thousands of them, some closed, isolate, self-contained and self-containing, others combining in open and fluid configurations of varied intimacy and range, and composing civilizations. Whether as simple cultures of simpler peoples or as complex civilizations of peoples more sophisticated, they seem related to the persons whose cultures and civilizations they are as the song is related to the bird that sings it, or the music is related to the swing band that produces it. Each manifests a character singular to itself—to many observers as distinct and contrasting as those of animal species—and as responsive to one another in much the same ways of indifference or curiosity, of flight or fight, of rivalry, submission or mastery, of mobile aggregation or selective association. Basically, all of them are built upon ways of begetting their kind and of securing food and clothing and shelter; of winning victories over illnesses and enemies, visible and invisible; of making the tools and weapons wherewith these things are done; and of saying and signifying the things and the doings. The last, their media and arts of communication, join them into a community presently remembering a common past and projecting a common future.

Such communities constitute the human condition, the details of which are the "problems" in "the meeting of the East and West"; in the impact of colonial powers and colonial peoples upon one another; in the influence of missionaries upon "natives" and "natives" upon missionaries; in the impact of "whites" upon the otherwise pigmented and the latter upon "whites"; in the relations between religious and cultural "minorities" and the "majorities" of which they are a part and apart (as the Irish have been in the United Kingdom, as the Flemings and Walloons in Belgium, or the northern Slavs and southern Slavs in their respective countries, or the Jews and the Arabs in the Middle East). The condition is the struggle of cultures for survival, world around. "Wars," declares the preamble to the charter of UNESCO, "are made in the minds of men," and the minds of men are made by their cultures, their ways of being together with each other in all their diversities of faiths and works, of earning their livings and living their lives, of remembering their dead and educating their living.

The base of these ways may indeed be universal. Their ground and goal may indeed be global. They may be—pundits of history and sociology have so described them—always and everywhere the same. But the stranger, first encountering another culture than his own, perceives neither the global ground nor the global goal. What first impresses him is its Otherness, the tangency and challenge of its immediate presence to his habits of being and doing. This strikes him first as a non-conformity, offering a violence to "right" conduct and "good order," which he may put down with laughter or beat up with condemnation. He may thus endeavor to obviate its obstruction to the accustomed flow of his consciousness, although the threat of its unknown danger compels him to stop, look, and listen. He is experiencing a thing alien, whose aliency is commensurable to the feelings of strangeness, the attitude of doubt and watchfulness, with which he responds to it. This total response of his, some psychologists declare, is primal and unlearned, the working of an instinct, not an insight. Even fully readied cultural anthropologists, set to manifest all sympathy and understanding, are said to respond so when they first join the culture they have selected for study; they being no more exempt from instinct than children or American politicians. The latter, of course, exaggerate and rationalize their mammalian xenophobia—if it be such—and make it into political capital; children merely outgrow it. One need not argue that it is a trait of our original nature antagonistic to the love of every out-group, to say nothing of the totality of out-groups which make up "mankind."

Nor need one argue that a lover of mankind neither does nor can envision the countless diverse and diversifying miscellany of human beings and their ways for which "mankind" is a name. No image that a painter could put on canvas or a sculptor shape in stone or metal could bring into a single conspectus those unending multiplicities. At best it could accomplish no more than does the word "mankind" itself—to serve as an incommensurate sign of that infinite variety. Nor has any poet or philosopher yet produced a definition adequate to those unnumbered constellations of cultures with their faiths, forms, and functions. On the record, the lover of mankind loves no actuality of all human existence as he loves his father or his mother or his lady fair, nor any artist's symbolization of that actuality. How, in the nature of things, can distributive mankind—and what other is visibly there?—be any man's experience either as perception or as image? How can his love be a love of the races of man as they are, where they are, and how they are?

Then what can, what does, the lover of mankind love?

The answers of tradition are varied. But whatever their import, their purport is some manner of nullifying the specific singularities of human beings, some manner of liquidating their diversities into identity, of consuming their individualities in sameness and their multitude in oneness. Their purport is a mankind always, everywhere, and everyhow the same. Love, indeed, could be accounted the energy which consummates this unification and presents the single identity.

Of what, with what?

Of the Other, the Alien, with the Self.

For to the tradition, otherness—aliency—is no good. To love is to condemn, to reject, or to destroy them; so to digest their strangeness as to render them of one flesh and one faith with oneself. To be other meant, among the ancient Greeks, to be barbarian; among the ancient Jews, to be Gentile; among the Christians of all times to be unbelievers and heretics. In the eyes of all, otherness was somehow a sin and a lie devoid of virtue and empty of worth; to love the Other was to make him of the same virtue and worth as the Self. So, in due course, the Greeks become hellenizers, the Jews judaizers, the Romans romanizers, the Christians christianizers, the Nazis nazifiers, the Communists communizers. "Soviet power," Stalin tells his hierarchy, "seeks to amalgamate all peoples into a single State union. . . . The existence of the Soviet Republic alongside of the imperialists is unthinkable. One or the other must triumph in the end." Each such lover of mankind purported to establish an empire of culture such as that for which Alexander set the first notable precedent; all endeavored with word and sword to reform the different in faith and works into a unity with themselves. Short of cannibalism, unification could only be free or forced conversion, a turn from cultural diversity to cultural univocality.

Because of this turn in the development of European man, the glory that was Greece and the grandeur that was Rome produced a humanistic civilization the working principles of which became a vision of man and nature that may have been used to rationalize imperial practices, but which nevertheless stood as the articles of a striving faith which Roman law and the entire cultural economy of the classical world made manifest. Initiative toward this vision had been taken by Socrates and Plato; they include Plato's idealization of the experiences of love.[1] Its full articulation was, however, the work of the Stoics, who in one context made "God" and "Love" but another language for the aid and comfort which man gives man. One need but recall a phrase of Pliny's lifted from some Greek Stoic: *"Deus est mortale juvari mortalem."* Zeno's *Republic* vividly contrasts with Plato's in that it envisages mankind as one world-city "of gods and men," all of whom are members of one another through the love which is the life-energy of nature, and the synonym of which is the *pronoia,* or providence of God. Stoic cosmopolitanism comprehended all the diversities of the human condition—from that of Epictetus, the slave, to that of Marcus Aurelius, the emperor—as inwardly one and the same. It included the dead and the unborn as well as the living, and it equated ascetic withdrawal from society and total commitment to society. It hypostatized a preferred human trait into a universal human essence. It made the demonstration of the essence the sign of salvation.

But Plato did indicate the gradient along which the Stoics evolved their philosophy, with its universal *humanum genus* a growth of nature according to nature's laws; its *humanitas* the excellence proper to this *genus* and likewise always and everywhere the same—outstandingly the same as reason, the *sapientia* of *Homo sapiens,* the energy of his powers of speech and arts of communication,[2] in the exercise, improvement, and perfection of which lives

[1] See especially *The Republic,* the *Symposium, Phaedrus;* but all the *Dialogues* carry the intent.
[2] See Cicero: *De Officiis.*

the communion that is the love of mankind. For the arts of communication are the means wherewith nature can be understood and employed in the service of men and men can realize their common humanity. They are the carriers of civilization, since that is but the unification of the diversities of men and the humanization of the non-human inwardness of things. People cease to be Hellenes and barbarians, Romans and provincials, patricians and proletarians, free men and slaves, to become one *humanity* with *humane* feelings for one another, and *humanitarian* attitudes. *Humanity* comes to designate not only the world's aggregate of men, women, and children, but also reciprocities of tenderness, compassion, and benevolence which might compose their communion and *ratio,* to be opposed to "man's inhumanity to man."

Another of the great traditional answers to our query: What does the lover of mankind love? derives from the Hebrews. This one translates the perceptual diversity and multiplicity of men into the oneness, Man, by means of supernatural revelation and commandment. It conceives existence as a stretch of time rather than a structure in space, and a function of changing purposes rather than of eternal law. For it, nature and man are the impotent creatures of an omnipotent creator, without whose sustaining power they collapse into nothing—a nothing which is likewise wickedness and sin and helplessness. To exist is to be a passing effect of the Everlasting Cause; hence, to know and love the Cause becomes an imperative of the struggle for survival. But the Cause can be known only if it chooses to be known; only if it reveals itself to its Effect; the effect has no power to seek it out. Revelation comes by Divine

Grace, not human desire; and it has come as the commandment to love the Revealer, so that the lover might go on living and growing. To love God is to obey him, and to obey him is to succeed in the struggle for survival; it is, hence, to love the Self which so struggles. This is not the same, however, as to love the other strugglers, even parents. Left to himself, the struggler does what the commandments forbid: he fears, hates, cheats, robs, slanders, envies, belies, curses, exploits. His existence is part of a war of all against all. It is this war that the Eternal Cause forbids to the passing Effect. His commandment is: "You shall love your neighbor as you love yourself; you shall love the alien as you love yourself." That is, the Other is to be treated as the Same; that which you love in him is that which you love in yourself; and ultimately that is the Eternal Cause of which you are both passing Effects. Since the visible Cause in a patriarchal society is a father according to the flesh, the invisible Cause becomes readily imaged as a universal Father according to the Spirit, through whose paternity all men are brothers. The transposition becomes "the fatherhood of God and the brotherhood of men," who are members of one another and love each other not as they are by and for themselves, but in and through the Oneness of the creative All-Father. . . .

Cognoscenti may regard the foregoing as no historically correct indication of the philosophic intent of the ordinances recorded in Leviticus, from the seventh century before the present era, and of the admonitions of the Hebrew prophets. I did not intend such an indication. What I have endeavored is to bring out a characteristic difference of attitude and object between the Hellenic and Hebraic ideas of "the love of mankind." The Graeco-Roman idea postulated an inward power, rationally self-directed toward its goal and consubstantial with it. The Hebraic idea envisaged an outward Creator commanding the rules of righteousness and in no way consubstantial with his commanded creature. Men could love God and one another, not in reason, but through revelation; not in accord with the eternal laws of nature, but in consequence of the miraculous grace of God.

The antithesis I have just set down is in historic fact far less apt to the ideals of a Hebrew or Judaist than to those of the Christian. It expresses the generic sentiment of the New Testament far more truly than that of the Old. It is the New Testament which communicates a certain climax of despair with men and the world, a feeling that its *humanum genus* was all sin, wickedness, and impotence, absolutely dependent on an Otherwordly Redeemer to bring it salvation from its own innate corruption. This feeling was far older than Christianity; it can be sensed in Plato, in the creeds of Diogenes and Epicurus and Zeno. All were less endeavors to change the facts than to turn the heart of man to such an apprehension of the facts as to enable him to endure them in serenity without illusion. By contrast, Christianity, in rite and rote vocal of the resentments and aspirations of imperial Rome's urban multitudes, became their ready syncretic symbol for their failure of nerve and thus the doctrine and discipline of a savior from the doom of this failure. To their sense of helplessness and of hopeless dependence on superior and arbitrary power came as truly good news the Christian assertion that it was a historic fact and not a cultist claim; that the mightiest of all such powers—the one God himself—so loved them that he chose to walk on earth as man and by his death on the cross to atone for the sin which was their very existence. To accept the atonement, to believe on the Christ, was to be born again out of the doom of death into eternal life of Oneness in Christ with the miscellany of the twice-born from everywhere. It was to become part of a total object of an Otherworldly love all outgoing generosity and grace unmotived, giving itself without return to save the beloved object from eternal death unto eternal life.

As the ancient civilization fell, as its order lapsed toward anarchy, its knowledge toward magic, its technics toward ritual, and its free communion became a congeries of mutually isolating hatreds and aggressions, this conception of love and love's object acquired a paramount importance. How could any mere creature dare to decline this love of the Omnipotent lover without meriting and receiving, also in this world, the suffering and death it was destined for in the Otherworld? To hate, to hunt down, and to destroy difference was the logical obverse to loving sameness. The history of Christianity as a religion of love is long the history of a sacerdotal imperialism with a program of hate and ruin for all who denied its totalitarian pretensions, and continues such in the greater part of the Christianized world. Communism has changed its symbols without altering its program.

That its struggles to consummate identification were frequently resisted; that the resistance formulated competing versions of the idea of divine love and its total object, led but to claims of infallibility by the catholicizing hierarchy. A philosophical and institutional reconstruction of these claims ensued upon the recovery, among the sacerdotal élite themselves, of the forgotten ideal of Humanity. The recoverers are known as Humanists. They were such, not alone because they valued the faith and works of classical antiquity above those of their Christian production. They were humanists also because they restored to the idea of Man the qualities of inward virtue, valor, and value which Christian despair had denied it. Among others, Rabelais, Montaigne, Leon Battista Alberti[3] signalize the restoration. It reaffirmed the *humanitas* of *humanum genus*.

By the last quarter of the seventeenth century Spinoza had completely reinstated man in nature and re-identified nature as God. He had redefined love as a substance of power. He could say that God loves himself with an infinite and perfect love and mean simply that the Universe is one, infinite, eternal, self-sustaining energy. He could argue that man's struggle for self-preservation is self-love as a mode of that unitary energy; that in loving himself man must needs love God as the intrinsic ground of his own survival, and that it is illusory to ask that God should love man in return. The last is an error that arises from love as blind passion and is dissipated when it becomes enlightened vision. This vision is man's passion transformed into man's understanding of the linkage of events which are grounds and conditions of his survival, the understanding which Spinoza terms "the intellectual love of God." Since, to any man the rest of mankind are the nearest constitutive part of that ineluctably belovèd Totality,

---

[3] See in Rabelais' account of the Abbey of Thélème: "Because free men, well-born, well-taught, holding conversations in honest groups, are by nature endowed with an instinct and incentive that always impels them to do virtuously and to withdraw from vice . . ." Montaigne doubts original sin and the need of grace. Alberti declares that "men can by their own power do anything they wish, if they really will it."

to love mankind becomes a rule of life for the enlightened self-interest in which self-preservation consummates itself. The diversities of human faiths and forms being but modes of the identity underlying, love enacts their mutual toleration in equal liberty and eventuates in free agreement.

It is no news that the humanistic insight penetrated the Protestant revision of Catholic doctrine concerning the nature of mankind and of the love which takes mankind for object. The trend was to preserve the transcendence and irreducible aliency of Creator to creature, but to regard the creature not as impotent and corrupt, but as independently possessing unalienable virtue, valor, and value. The age which followed Spinoza's is called the Age of Enlightenment. Its representative theology is called Deism. This abolishes the traditional Christian antithesis between the City of God—a perfect society of the saved—and the City of the World—the society of the natural man, all sin, corruption, and eternal death. It develops the vision of one Cosmopolis, the citizens of which, under the laws of nature and nature's God, need neither Saviour nor the miracle of grace to accomplish their salvation, but are able by their own vision and work to save themselves. Their salvation is a necessary effect of which they are the sufficient causes. It is a result of the knowledge which is power that they have themselves developed by studying nature and the human nature which is one of nature's formations. Salvation, hence, follows from insight into the dynamics of things and thoughts. It is the same as discovering and creating knowledge, conserving knowledge, using and transmitting knowledge. It is self-wrought, and its processes are observable among all sorts and conditions of men. The love of mankind becomes the endeavor to free them from the fetters in which authoritarian powers claiming divine right have bound them.

This, by and large, is what such spokesmen of the Enlightenment as Voltaire, Kant, Condorcet, Paine, and Jefferson believed. Its ultimate personal statement is Paine's: "The world is my country; to do good, my religion." Its representative collective statement is the American Declaration of Independence.[4] August Comte's "religion of humanity" clothes it in authoritarian trappings adapted from Catholicism. He expounds humanity as the true God, the *Grand Être* that every man must love and obey with a total love, taught and directed by a hierarchy of a positivist élite, who are to be the science-inspired priests of that Great Being.

The church Comte founded became one more cult among the multitude increasing and multiplying during the nineteenth century, with little influence and less power. But the humanist sentiment which generated it and so many others is still far from the height of its creative flood. The word *humanity* became, as Sir Henry Maine observed, its sign and carrier.[5] Certainly the life of it continues to be what earlier times called "love." But during

[4] "Man," Paine wrote in *The Rights of Man,* "acquired a knowledge of his rights by attending justly to his interests, and discovers in the event that the strength and powers of despotism consist wholly in the fear of resisting it, and that in order to be free, it is sufficient that he wills it." The Communists are excommunicating the *aficionados* of this philosophy as heretics guilty of "cosmopolitanism."

[5] "The notion of what for want of a better phrase I must call a moral brotherhood of the whole human race has been gaining ground during the whole course of history and we have now a large abstract term answering to this notion—Humanity." *Early History of Institutions, 1875.*

the nineteenth and twentieth centuries that word was displaced by less invidious and more specific names for the affirmative relations among the people who together compose humanity. The revolutionary triad, "liberty, equality, fraternity," carries the same sentiment. "Democracy" is their abbreviation and names a cause that is advanced and defended by every art of peace and war against all manner of despotisms—feudal, sacerdotal, racial, political, economic, intellectual, esthetic. The creative terms of such advance and defense are the struggles—to abolish slavery (notably the American Civil War), to improve health, to achieve general abundance in ideas as well as possessions, by multiplying and safeguarding civil liberties, to secure and defend the peace by collective action—which signalize the global history. And they signalize especially the Western civilization of the two centuries past. Their most recent projection as operational organization is the United Nations; as ideal, its Universal Declaration of Human Rights. From the American Declaration of Independence to this global Declaration, history has been made upon a gradient of will and vision—whereon the men who made it have not counted the costs—that may be rightly denoted as "love of mankind."

But it is significant that the more nearly this love came to consummation in action, the less the term figured in discourse. Today's usage tends to restrict the word "love" to the modes of sexual behavior, to the esoteric intentions of the theologians and the metaphysicians, and to such compenetrations of them as Freud ruminates in *Das Behagen in der Kultur*.

Moreover, to the believing democrat, Mankind or Humanity does not convey the same meaning as to the positivist or the sacerdotal totalitarian. His total object of love is a different object. It is not a concept or universal which renders differences indifferent or sinks them in sameness. It is not a One which consumes diversity in identity. When the democrat declares "all men are created equal" and so forth, he is not affirming the identity of the different and the unreality of their differences; he is affirming at once the reality and the parity of human differences. He is affirming the equal right of the different to live, to be free, to seek happiness, *as* different. Mankind for him is the configuration of the miscellany of different persons and peoples; it is the concrete ways by which each—the peer of the others in its own singularity of valor, virtue, and value—orchestrates itself to all the others—*e pluribus unum*. The love of mankind is thus, for the democrat, enlightened devotion to the mutual guarantees that different men and societies give each other for the equal liberty and security of their personal and cultural individualities; it is their reciprocities of self-preservation. Democratic love of mankind practices neither tolerance nor intolerance, neither grants to nor withholds from the Other, his equal right to freedom and safety. It simply acknowledges this equality of the Other and seeks, in helping him to live and to grow, to live more abundantly itself.[6]

[6] See Mr. Paul Hoffman, in his address to the *Institute of World Affairs* at Riverside, California, December 11, 1951: "We have got to turn our backs on hate and fear in this country of ours and show the world dramatically that the government of the people, for the people, and by the people, is the only government which gives the people the opportunity to grow and develop to their fullest capacity."

See Thomas Paine, *The Rights of Man,* 1792: "If there is a country in the world where concord, according to common calculation would be least expected, it is America. Made up, as it is, of people from dif-

Usage suggests that loves are qualitatively different, and that discourse identifies or distinguishes them according to the problem it is resolving. English has but this one word for a considerable variety of relationships. Such terms as *amity, friendship,* are not regarded as equivalents. Hebrew is here as poor as English; it has no alternates for *ahavah.* But ancient Greek owns at least three major terms: *eros, philia, agapé;* and classical Latin gives us *amor* and *caritas* —perhaps *cupiditas* should also be counted in. From the Greek and Latin English speech builds up words in numbers, specific to particular ideas—words, for example, such as *philanthropy,* which once literally meant "love of mankind." But a philanthropist is today a rich man who gives large sums of money to be expended on specific goods and services for needy people who are to him just so many *x*'s in a social equation. His philanthropy is neither personal nor passionate; it is a reaction against abstract evils rather

---

ferent nations, accustomed to different forms and habits of government, speaking different languages, and more different in their modes of worship, it would appear that the union of such a people would be impracticable; but by the simple operation of constructing government on the principles of society and the rights of man, every difficulty retires and all the parts are brought into cordial unison. . . . There, government is not a private trade but a public trust; it of itself has no rights; they are only duties." Regarding slavery, Paine said (*African Slavery,* 1775) it was as immoral as "murder, robbery, lewdness and barbarity." He urged Americans to "discontinue and renounce it with grief and abhorrence." Since the Protestant Reformation "all distinction of nations and privileges of one above others, are ceased. Christians are taught to account all men their neighbors and love their neighbors as themselves; and do to all men as they would be done by; to do good to all men; and manstealing is ranked with enormous crime." How can the slave trade and slavery be squared with this teaching?

than an enthusiasm for concrete goods. George Eliot once called such a person "one whose charity increases directly as the square of the distance." She meant by *charity*, of course, what we more and more mean: gifts of goods and services to such as beg for them (panhandlers) or to such as need them (clients of charitable organizations). But the word *charity* has also other meanings. The more nearly persistent one is that intended in Paul's admonitions to his Corinthians—the charity that "beareth all things, believeth all things, hopeth all things, endureth all things ... never faileth,"[7] and is greater than faith and hope. In the Vulgate, the word is *caritas,* in Greek *agapé;* and modern translations of the New Testament render it *love.* As Paul signalizes this *love,* it is of a nature quite other than *philia* and *eros,* though of what nature depends more on the interests and loyalties of Paul's interpreters than on any objective realization of the Apostle's own difficulties with his Corinthians. In its latest New Testament use, *love* is made the same as God (*God is love*) and *loving* the same as *knowing God.* But never immanently, never directly; always through the mediation of the divine Son, of Him who is the *caritas* of the angry Father, who is God-as-man, loving man and thus redeeming him from his deadly human Otherness. And it is only in and through the unmerited grace of this "at-onement-working" divine love that mankind is able not to hate, but to love one another and to be at one with one another in the communion which the agapetic feast signalizes. This union is beyond the power of their humanity. It is the consummation of love regarded as a metaphysical substance and a theological virtue,

[7] I Cor. XIII: 1-13.

having nothing in common with what goes for love in nature and in human relations. It is transubstantiation and hypostasis of that natural love. "Love, as the New Testament intends it," declares the neo-orthodox theologian Brunner, "is impossible to man; it is possible to God alone." It is divine mercy repressing divine justice; divine grace forgiving the Otherness of the human Other; taking it—disobedience, sin, unreality and all—up into its own blissful reality. It is the Christ as total condescension, the charity of infinite worth toward infinite worthlessness; moving from its own zenith to that nadir of aliency in order to lift it up into existence and inspire it with faith in its own good will to man. Yet it is not this alone. A hatred accompanies it, corresponding to its own agapetic scope and intensity. Its provident love requires a "resurrection unto condemnation" as well as unto salvation; and a blessedness of the beloved (the communion of Saints), whose perfection is also an exercise in contemplative sadism, exemplified on earth as the chastening of the Other in faith by the Church universal and militant which embodied this love. It is love at once totalitarian rather than total and authoritarian rather than authoritative. Not to submit and accept it is to reject mercy and merit "justice" as auto-da-fé.

The antithesis to this condescending love is that aspiring love the processes and products of which are a progression toward effects ever more excellent than itself. The Greek word for the latter is *eros*. Broadly, it stands for the energy of creation and reason which Plato somewhat ambiguously signalizes. It is not the energy of a descent but of an ascent. *Eros* is that drive in the human psyche which it *uses* in the creation of its works of progress, which it has *used up* at last when it attains to the vision of the Idea of the

Good and the Eternal Ideas that it implies. Freud, in a transposition of the Christian concepts of which he seems unaware, employs *eros* to denote inherent creative energy in constant strife with an equally inherent instinct toward the inorganic immobility which is organic death. An analogous transposition, consciously made, however, is sketched by Charles Pierce,[8] who imagines the entire universe as a process in which cosmos evolves itself from chaos, order from chance, habit from accident; and in which the creative energy, generating the new from the old, yet holds the two harmoniously together. This energy Pierce calls love, evolutionary love. But the Greek word that he employs to signalize his vision is not *eros;* it is *agapé*—the energy of attraction and expansion—that generates particulars and joins them to one another in ever-expanding generality, making of that communion a community of habit and idea —including God—which binds individuals to one another, yet points beyond any and all of their singularities to the general humanity which they are. For Pierce's *tychistic agapism* (or agapeticism) the love of mankind would be the generative force of the unitary idea of mankind. Hatred and evil would be undeveloped stages of the developing energy of this universal love, which is always reaching out beyond itself to an unknown Other, an outgrowth genuinely novel that it at the same time harmonizes to itself.

The event that evolution, that growth, that creation, are each a transition from the known to the unknown, may have its symbol in the fable that Cupid, the God of Love, is blind. It could imply also that the love of mankind is, in

[8] See *Chance, Love and Logic,* Part II (edited by Morris R. Cohen) and *Collected Papers of Charles Sanders Pierce,* Vol. VI, "Scientific Metaphysics."

a specific person sincerely moved by this sentiment, the love of loving, which fixes on no object but may attach itself to any. This notion of the ideo-motor stance that the word *love* denotes to the psychologist might get a certain color of plausibility from the kinship that English philology assigns to the word. For on the one side, it is joined to the Sanskrit *lubh,* which means desire, and to the Latin *lubet* or *libet,* which means *it pleases;* on the other side, it is joined to the Teutonic *lub,* the Anglo-Saxon *leóf;* it signalized *having liefer;* it goes with *lief* and *believe* and involves *liberty.* These relationships provide a philological ground for Freud's associating love with what he calls the pleasure-principle and theologians call "blessedness." But they indicate also that loving is the self-preservation of the state of being pleased, of well-being, theologically, the perfection of well-being, and that far from starting primarily as hunger or craving, it starts as an abundance, which empties and continues as a diversified self-repletion. The human relations through which this is achieved may be simple and few or complex and multitudinous. When they are postulated as guides for action, they suffuse the natal ideo-motor stance with their own substance and shadow. But the natal stance is nuclear, and diverse as may be the traits of the love of mankind of which it is the vital center, it determines whether this love is consummated by destroying and consuming the integrity of the Other, or by preserving and cherishing his singularity. This is the issue between Totalitarianism and Democracy.

The Love of God

James Luther Adams

The Love of God

James Luther Adams

In the largely secularized culture and language of our time, the subject of this chapter is by no means one that elicits universal interest. To many serious-minded people phrases such as "the love of God," "God's love for man," or "man's response to God's love" are almost meaningless. Yet the subject is actually one of universal concern. This is obscured by the fact that we often discuss it without using theological language and perhaps even without being fully aware of what we are doing.

Even among people who think of themselves as having made a religious commitment, one may not discuss our subject without considerable difficulty. The variety of religious traditions and affiliations in our society create almost as many semantic problems as are confronted in face of the "unbelievers." In addition, the sharp differences of religious outlook that prevail among Jews and Christians present a host of difficulties with respect to both language and content.

Taking this situation into account, the ensuing discussion will assume no explicitly religious commitment on the part of the reader. Therefore, we must as it were begin at the beginning; and we shall go scarcely beyond that beginning.

At the outset an attempt will be made to show that, contrary to the rather generally accepted view, the basic concerns of religion are inescapable; indeed that some sort of religious faith is found among all men. Thus the most significant differences between people will be interpreted not as differences between religion and irreligion but as differences between conceptions of faith and also of the love of God; ultimately, the basic issue concerns the question as to what the most reliable object of human devotion is. Finally, an attempt will be made to show that the decisive differences between conceptions of the love of God become most clear when we determine the social-institutional implications of these conceptions.

I

The very title of the present chapter will arouse hostility in some minds. Love of family, of friends, of country—these are loves that may be, and often are, frustrate or perverse. No one, however, doubts the reality of these objects of devotion. It is not so with "the love of God." For some readers the word "God" is not the sign of a reality but of a powerful illusion; it epitomizes all that belongs to the pathology of love and dreams. From this viewpoint, the only appropriate intent of the present discussion should be to expose the illusion.

Such an attitude may not properly be brushed aside. The God that is rejected by the "unbeliever" may be an illusion and wholly worthy of rejection. After all, a multitude of conceptions of God, and of the love of God, has appeared in the history of religion; not all of them can possibly be true. Many of these illusions are doggedly tenacious. The absolute sanction of authoritarian faith (both religious and secular) and of the security it affords, protects it from radical criticism; and non-authoritarian faiths have their own ways of ignoring criticism, too.

Those people who are hostile to religion will not find themselves alone in their critical attitude. In much that they reject they bear the heritage of a venerable company of religious men. From even before the times of Amos and Plato there have been prophets, philosophers, and theologians who have devoted a supreme effort to unmasking the illusions of uncritical religion.

But there is also such a thing as uncritical irreligion. The rejection of all belief in God as illusory may be the consequence of a failure to consider conceptions of God more plausible than those rejected. In some instances, moreover, the rejection of belief in God issues from the false notion that theology and religious faith are possible only because people indulge in speculation on questions for which no dependable answers are available. This view can often find cogent justification. But this rejection of so-called speculation is itself a spurious speculation. It may be tied up with an illusion, the illusion that religious faith as such may be dispensed with.

Actually, the nonreligious are not themselves without faith, even though they reject what they call speculation. There are many kinds of faith that may be dispensed with. But there remains one kind which no man can live without. We do not need to use the word "faith" to refer to it. The word "confidence" will serve just as well. No man and no culture can for long maintain a dynamic and creative attitude toward life without the confidence that human life has some important meaning either actual or potential, and that this meaning may in some tolerable fashion be maintained or achieved, in other words, that resources are available for the fulfillment of this meaning. This concern with the meaning of life and with the resources available is no merely optional luxury. It is a universal concern among men. It is the essential concern of religion. In its characteristic intention religion has to do with these inescapable issues and realities, and unless we are coming to terms with these issues our concern is not essentially religious. To be sure, what calls itself religion can be a means for attempting to evade these issues. Irreligion is often a protest against trivial or perverted religion, it may be a way of coming to terms with the serious and inescapable issues. Archbishop Temple perhaps had this fact in mind when he asserted, "It is a great mistake to suppose that God is only or even chiefly concerned with religion."

If we understand the word "religion" to refer to the concern with the inescapable issues regarding the meaning and the fulfillment of life, we may say that there is no such thing as a completely irreligious person. Both the "non-religious" and the "religious" person are concerned with these issues, and they are both somehow believers; they are people of faith, whether they use the word "God" or not. Indeed, the rejection of the word "God" may be only a sign that the word does not point to the ground of faith or confidence. The rejection itself may reveal confidence of some sort; it is a sign of devotion.

Man lives by his devotions. He lives by his love for his god. All alike place their confidence in something, whether it be in human nature, reason, scientific method, church, nation, Bible, or God. This confidence finds explicit or implicit expression in belief and disbelief. As Emerson observed, "A man bears beliefs as a tree bears apples."

To equate the devotion one lives by with the love of God may seem at first blush to be questionable. Is this not a mere playing with words? Does not this imply, for example, that an atheist who is utterly devoted to his atheism is thereby expressing his love for God? And is this not absurd?

The absurdity lies only on the surface. It is no mere word play to assert that the convinced atheist loves God, particularly if his atheism grows out of a total attitude toward life. He who with seriousness rejects belief in God (as he understands that word) expresses loyalty to a standard of truth or of goodness which he lives by; he believes this truth or goodness is valid and reliable. For him this truth or goodness is sacred; it may not be violated. The atheist rejects what appears to be sacred and sovereign for the theist; but in doing so he recognizes something else that is sovereign and even holy for him. This recognition of something as sovereign, in practice if not in theory, appears in both the serious atheist and the serious theist. The one rejects the word "God," and the other accepts it. But both believe something is sovereign and reliable.

Sacred, sovereign, reliable. Just these are the qualities that have always been associated with deity. It would appear that even when belief in God ostensibly disappears, the attributes of deity remain and are attached to something that is not called "God." Religion therefore might say to the unbeliever, "When me you fly, I am the wings." In other words, if we discover what a person really believes to be sovereign, what he will cling to as the principle or reality without which life would lose its meaning, we shall have discovered his religion, his god. This sovereign object of devotion is not always readily discernible, but it can sometimes be detected by what we might call the "temperature test." When the temperature of a person's mind or spirit rises to defend something to the very last ditch, then generally that person's sacred devotion is at stake. The test is as revealing when applied to the believer in God as when applied to the unbeliever. It may show that the God avowed by the believer is not really sacred to him. It can show also that a serious rejection of belief in God may be a form of the love of God in the sense that it is a giving of oneself to, an identification with, something cherished above all else.

This kind of atheism is really a happy, confident atheism. It is in its way an affirmation of meaning. There is another kind of atheism, however, which is far from confident or happy. It denies that there is anything worthy of ultimate loyalty, that there is anything sacred or sovereign. This kind of atheism is nihilism, it takes nothing (not even itself) seriously; it holds that nothing is worthy of love and that love itself is meaningless. This is the anomie that leads to suicide. This perhaps is the only consistent atheism. It asserts that nothing dependable remains.

Whether one calls himself theist or atheist, the issue comes down to this: What is sacred? What is truly sovereign? What is ultimately reliable? These are the questions that are involved in every discussion of the love of God. And even if one does not like to use the words "the love of God," he will nevertheless deal with these questions in any discussion of the meaning of human existence. These are the questions to which we are always giving the answers in the embracing patterns and the ultimate decisions of our existence. Indeed, the struggle between the different answers constitutes the very meaning of human history.

II

Nihilism, the sense of complete meaninglessness in life, is by no means rare in our time of troubles. It appears today on a large scale in certain parts of Europe where the carnage and destruction of world war have left in their wake thousands of refugees and displaced persons crouching in despair in the rubble. One can today see hundreds of these refugees crowded into the camps of Berlin. Emptiness is in their eyes, and in their stomachs, and in their hearts. Many other people who are not refugees share this despair as they clear away the rubble and go on reburying the dead who are only now being unearthed. "What is the use," they ask, "if the end of our rebuilding is again to be mass murder and rubble?" This nihilism is not to be found alone in Germany. I recall hearing Arnold Toynbee say that, if the nations are not able to prevent war now for at least a generation, many people in England might prefer to surrender to the enemy and submit even to a dictatorship rather than go to war again.

Nor is the nihilism of despair confined to the savagely war-torn countries. It issues also out of the social dislocations of modern city life. It is met every day by the psychiatrist and the minister in their offices and in the increasing number of institutions required for the treatment of this illness.

The essence of this nihilism has been vividly depicted by the French existentialist Jean-Paul Sartre in his play *No Exit*. The scene of this play is hell, the hell of isolation.

The author depicts the inferno of human loneliness and despair, the alienation of three souls—a man who had in life been a fascist collaborationist, and two women, the one a strumpet and the other a Lesbian. They are all three imprisoned and condemned to the eternal torture of keeping each other company. For them there is *no exit* from the torture of loneliness even though they are together. They share no common values that can give them dignity either as individuals or as a group locked in their room in hell. The souls in Dante's Inferno retain some human dignity; they seem to be at least worthy of punishment. But the souls in Sartre's hell have lost even that dignity. The three people struggle for each other's attention but without believing they have anything worth giving and without believing the others would really esteem anything worth giving. In the end, the man cannot decide whether his own spiritual leprosy allies him most closely with the woman who has been and still is a strumpet or with the one who is a pervert. And yet all of them are to remain for eternity without any other companions and without any affectionate, human interest in each other. Finally, in desperation the man says, "There's no need for hot pokers in this place. Hell is—other people." The "hell" represented in the play is the "hell" of sitting out eternity in common isolation from one another, again and again making abortive attempts at forming tolerable relationships, or at destroying one another.

The anti-heroes of *No Exit* live in the void of meaninglessness, for meaning is a shared and enjoyed relatedness. They participate in nothing that forms community. The only thing human that remains in them is the longing for community. Man is made for fellowship, and without it he is of all creatures the most miserable. In this play, then, we have a parable of the human condition, a parable of an inescapable reality. The condition of man—that he is made for fellowship—is a fact that he cannot elude. He belongs to a cosmos that is social. Only the despairing nihilist has lost the sense of belonging to it. The confident atheist, in finding some meaning in life (even though it be partly expressed in his "atheism"), has the sense of belonging to a community. He even places his confidence somehow in that community. But in doing so he does not characteristically think of himself as a man of faith. He simply takes the community, and also its possibilities, for granted.

The theist believes of course that he belongs to a community of meaning; but he believes also that this community is not ultimately man's own, either in its actuality or its possibilities. He believes that as a human being, he possesses some freedom to choose the ways in which he will participate or not participate in the social cosmos in which he finds himself. But for him, the condition of man as a creature longing for fellowship and as a creature possessing some freedom is a gift. In religious parlance, it is a gift of divine grace. His fulfillment of his freedom is seen also as a divinely given task—and peril.

Here a positive parable of the divinely given community of meaning, the parable of the prodigal son, may with profit be added to Sartre's parable regarding the negation of community. The latter is a parable of the lost community; the former a parable of the community lost and found again.

The parable of the prodigal son is not primarily an ethical parable teaching right behavior. It is, we might say, a metaphysical parable, a picture of the social cosmos of divinely given community, of the divinely given human freedom, and of the divinely given task to fulfill that freedom in all its venture and risk. In short, this is a parable of the nature of existence and meaning, and of the love of God—of His love for man and of man's response to that love.

It is not possible or necessary here to spell out all the significant details of the parable. But we should observe that its principal religious import resides in the parable as a whole—in its assertion that the total condition of man is to be understood as a manifestation of God's love and that participation in community is man's responding love for God. Each of the elements of the parable must be understood in this context, the dignity of the creature by virtue of its participation in the social cosmos, the community of relatedness in freedom ("Give me my portion," says the son), the isolation and frustration that issue from the breaking of fellowship, the possibility of new beginning, the enrichment and fulfillment of community that comes from reconciliation. And we should add that this whole picture depicts not only the loss and the regaining of community on the part of the son; it presents, in the image of the father, the attitude of love which men must take toward each other in the re-formation and transformation of community.

It is just at this point that our earlier questions become pertinent. We have suggested that we may determine anyone's conception of the love of God (including the atheist's) by answering the questions: What is sacred for him? What is considered sovereign, what the reliable object of devotion? If we pose these questions in relation to the parable of the Prodigal Son, we may secure highly significant answers. But this will require that we take note of another figure in the story. So significant is he in this parable that it has been often suggested that the story should be named "the parable of the Elder Son."

The elder son in the parable corresponds to the antihero of Sartre's play. He manages not only to lose participation in community; he also fails to regain it. But here the resemblance stops. His failure is due to the fact that he is a "good" man. He does the evil as well as the good that "good" men do. He does remain at home, and (unlike the prodigal) he helps to maintain the fabric of the community. But when the prodigal returns, the brother becomes the defender of morality, of law and order. He makes his ethical principles sacred and sovereign. But they turn out to be unreliable, for they would make the community exclusive; they have in them nothing that goes out to greet the prodigal who has come to himself and wants to be a part of the community again. In the mind of the teacher of the parable, the sovereign good, the sovereign reality, is not an ethical law. It is the outgoing power that transforms and fulfills the law; it is the creative element in the law which prevents justice from becoming self-righteous and unjust. But it cannot work here because it is resisted by the "good" man. And the consequence is that the "good" man is undone; he becomes alienated in isolation from the affectional community. He depends upon something undependable.

The love of God, then, is the giving of oneself to that power which holds the world together and which when we are tearing it apart persuades us to come to ourselves and start on new beginnings; it is not bound to achieved evil, and it is not bound to achieved good. The prodigal escaped from the one, the elder brother was bound to the other.

And why is this sort of love alone reliable? Because it alone has within it the seeds of becoming, even in the face of tragedy and death—when it keeps confidence, saying, "Into thy hands I commend my spirit." This love is reliable also because it alone can engender respect and love for the necessary diversity of men. Through this love which is a self-giving to a process of transformation rather than to a "law," men, in their relation to each other and in their diversity, become mutually supporting and enhancing rather than mutually impoverishing. Here the antagonism between egoism and altruism is transcended in the devotion to the good of others which is at the same time the fulfillment of the good of the self. In the fellowship of the love of God one loses his life to find it. And yet the loss and the finding are more than the process of self-realization. Man becomes a new creature. This is the work of God that brings the self to something more than and beyond the self, beyond even the "highest self."

This kind of love, however, promises no rosy path. It may lead to what Thomas à Kempis calls "the royal way of the cross," a way which God as well as man traverses, not for the sake of suffering in itself to be sure, but for the sake of suffering, separated mankind. A comprehending mutuality rooted in immemorial being stirs and affirms itself anew to heal and unite what has been wounded and separated.

I have never seen this re-creative power of love in its full orb portrayed more tellingly than in a sixteenth-century woodcut titled "The Prodigal Son," which used to be kept in the Dürer Museum in old Nuremberg. In this picture the father and the son, with joy and suffering in their faces, are almost at the point of reuniting on the road that leads home. Their arms are extended toward each other, but the two have not yet embraced. Yet out beyond them we see their shadows extending as it were into the depth of being. And there they are already embracing. The two had always belonged together. They belonged together in something antecedently given to man, as on the day of creation when the morning stars sang together and all the sons of God shouted for joy. The reuniting of the separated is a re-creation, and thereby a new creation.

The love of God, then, is a love that man cannot give unless he has first received it. Ultimately, it is not even his to give, for it is not in his keeping. It is in the keeping of a power that men can never fully know, of a power that they must in faith trust. Man's expression of it is a response to an antecedent glory and promise, the ground of meaning and the ever new resource for its fulfillment.

III

"By their fruits shall ye know them" is obviously a test that must be applied to men's love for God. We learn what is meant by any conception of the love of God by observing what sort of behavior issues from it. Indeed, the principal way to make a religious-ethical idea clear is to show what differences it makes in action. This test of the meaning of an idea we commonly apply in the realm of personal behavior. Love for God, we say, which does not issue in individual integrity, in humility, and in affectionate concern for others, is counterfeit.

But the meaning of love for God must be clarified in another realm besides that of personal attitude and behavior.

It becomes fully clear—and relevant—only when we know what it means for institutional behavior, when we know what kind of family, or economic system, or political order it demands. The decisive differences between the old Lutherans and the Quakers, for example, may not be immediately discerned from their words about the love of God, but they become sharply clear in their different conceptions of the family. The one group sanctioned a sort of patriarchal family in which the authoritarian father was the Vicar of God in the home, and love of God among the children was supposed to produce instant, unquestioning obedience; the other group preferred a family in which a more permissive, persuasive atmosphere prevailed. Yet both groups avowed the love of God as proclaimed in the Gospels. In general, then, we may say that the meaning of a religious or ethical imperative becomes concrete when we see it in relation to the social context in which it operates. Often the meaning of an ethical generality can be determined by observing what its proponents wish to change in society or to preserve unchanged.

Recently in Greece I visited the remarkable Byzantine church of the eleventh century at Daphni, situated on the ancient Sacred Way from Athens to Eleusis. As one emerges from the vestibule into the main church and as the eyes meet the imposing and striking mosaics on the walls of the old monastic church, one senses immediately in this monumental style of Eastern Christendom a powerful feeling for the sacred and the sovereign, the majestic and the commanding. The eye rises to the dome and one is awestruck by the grim King of Heaven, the All-Ruler (Pantocrator), surrounded by the cruciferous nimbus, holding in His left hand the Book and with His right hand blessing the worshippers. The commanding energy of Christ the Pantocrator in his high eminence above the mosaics of the Prophets and the Feasts of the Church recalls to the worshippers the familiar themes of salvation. But in its time this Pantocrator symbolized also a political idea, the absolute authority and the majestic unapproachability of the Emperor. The authority of the Pantocrator was understood in terms of the rule of the Emperor. The one buttressed the other. The church and its God have become a department of the absolute state.

Here was little freedom apart from that narrow and insignificant margin permitted by the Emperor-Pantocrator. To the modern man accustomed to the democratic way of life, or to anyone who esteems the community of mutuality and freedom reflected in the parable of the prodigal son, this Caesaro-papism is demonic. The contrast between the King of Heaven (and Emperor) in the mosaic and the Father in the parable highlights opposite ends of the spectrum of conceptions of the love of God.

All the more striking is the contrast if one recalls that the primitive church, the social organization that emerged from the Gospels (which, to be sure, was not a democracy in any modern sense), gave a new dignity to Everyman— to the fisherman, to the slave, to woman, and even to the prodigal. The new fellowship enhanced this dignity by eliciting a new freedom from its members and by assigning them unprecedented responsibility. But, as the Byzantine outcome illustrates, this new freedom and responsibility were soon to be threatened and were later to be submerged.

It is beyond the scope of our discussion here to attempt to apply the spirit and the norms of the love of God (as characterized all too briefly in these pages) to the contemporary situation. Our purpose at this juncture is only to propose that belief in God and the love of God must, as Whitehead has observed regarding the early Christian conceptions, become the basis for principles of social action and organization. This means that those who interpret the love of God as movement toward a community of freedom and mutuality will be able to vindicate the claim that they serve a power that is reliable, only by yielding to that power in the midst of a world that is suffering, divided by the cleavages of race, class, and nation. What is at stake is the creation of a world in which this kind of love of God becomes incarnate in a more just and free society.